ENDORSEMENTS

"CJ Powers is a gifted communicator who has the ability to provide great content in an interesting and engaging manner. "

Bill Snider – *Director, Asia Pacific Media Ministry*

"CJ has made filmmaking and story structure his passion and lifelong course of study. Consequently, he has become a master at both."

Guy Cote – *Author and Screenwriter*

"If you're looking for valuable insights into the craft of filmmaking, count on CJ to deliver. His writing is like a great movie you want to watch again and again because each time you find something new to enhance your own productivity."

Paul Munger – *Screenwriter/Producer*

"From skilled storyteller, to visual director, CJ shares what it takes to create intriguing scenes, multi dimensional characters, and visual stories that engage the viewer and bring life (and perhaps awards) to your craft!"

Francine Locke – *Award Winning Actress*

"CJ is one of the best prepared and conscientious directors in the market place. He has a creative vision in mind well before the camera ever rolls, shares his ideas, is open to input from crew, and has the ability to mix the talents of everyone on the shoot so the right product ends up on the screen."

Frank Loose – *Director of Photography*

Notes from the Napkin

A Director's Cut on Filmmaking

CJ Powers

Notes from the Napkin: A Director's Cut on Filmmaking

By CJ Powers

Printed in USA

Published by Powers Productions, Inc.

Manufactured in the United States of America

ISBN: 978-0-9799294-3-4

Dedication

To the One who made me creative

and gave me a passion for film…

To the screenwriters and filmmakers

that have supported my blog and e-zine

articles over the past few years…

And to Lisa England, who inspired me

to help writing/film students master their craft

as they explore the human condition through the arts.

ACKNOWLEDGEMENTS

I want to thank the tribe of filmmakers, students, fans and youth workers that have made my blog successful. Seldom do authors enjoy such wonderful support of their work and ideas. Your encouragement helped my writing efforts be more valuable to my readers and me.

While I'm amazed that it took me three previous books before I finally wrote one on filmmaking, I'm delighted to have taken the step to share information others have generously shared with me.

I'm very thankful to the famous and not-so-famous film industry professionals that have taken time to share their key insights that have molded the way I work my craft.

A special *thank you* goes out to Fran Eaton for her wonderful editing. The hard work and laughs were well worth it.

And, I must once again thank my dad for letting me use his 16mm camera when I was in grade school and his daily reminders of how to tell a story through *showing* the story, not *telling* it.

Table of Contents

INTRODUCTION

Since I started writing my blog, CJ's Corner, I've been asked questions by hundreds of filmmakers. Some were into film and others, television. Some were beginners, eager to learn. Others were professional, just wanting to find one Easter egg in our encounter for their tool belt. With all the differences in filmmakers, they all held one thing in common: They wanted a golden nugget from another filmmaker's experience.

I, too, am a person that thrives on learning from others, especially learning those little tips that work extremely well not covered in most university courses and industry books. I'll never forget the day my daughter, who at the time of this writing is working on her fourth feature film, told me that after four years of film classes she hadn't really learned anything new, and found herself on numerous occasions teaching film staff.

This wasn't to say my daughter's university didn't know film or how to teach it. Rather, her upbringing put her in front of enough productions and experienced professionals - including her proud father - that she was able to find numerous Easter eggs for her tool belt that made class seem basic and mundane.

The richest golden nuggets I've found have come from professionals during passing, off-the-cuff moments. The conversations weren't planned and the professionals hadn't memorized any key words or elevator speeches, but instead shared spontaneously from their hearts on filmmaking. The good news is their comments came just in time for me to take advantage of that specific piece of information.

The first Easter egg of directing knowledge I found was in high school. I had come across a fan book of the stars that had addresses and phone numbers in it. Just for the fun of it, I called film director and actor Ron Howard. He was surprised that his contact information was in the book and made sure it was removed the next day.

However, Howard did honor my phone call and allowed me to ask him several questions. I asked questions about directing that may have been trivial for him, but greatly changed my thinking and my future. Although, I'll never forget his response to a comment I made. He actually found an Easter egg in our conversation for his own tool belt. He was clearly a director devoted to learning from any source he came across.

My next phone call was to Ken Burns, one of the greatest documentarians of our time. Surprisingly he, too, was very helpful and shared a tip that enlightened me on how to get my first movie funded. It was no surprise that my first CBS documentary, Chileda - Children at Work, developed only two years later, when I was 18 years old.

Phone calls weren't the only way I gathered these precious nuggets of knowledge. I picked up the vast majority of notes at networking events or on film sets. Whether it was during breaks, meals or over cocktails, most of those treasured moments lasted no more than two to five minutes. Afterwards I often quickly sketched those ideas on the back of napkins – hence, the title for this book.

Based on all the questions I've been asked of filmmakers, I've decided to write this book, one napkin at a time. Each chapter is an answer to a question that I've asked or was asked of me. Since most of the answers were actually jotted on napkins, I've titled the book appropriately.

The chapters should take you only two to five minutes to digest, the same amount of time I had to take the information in.

Happy Easter egg hunting!

Working an Idea into a Viable Script

Creating the Idea

Every film starts with an idea. It's a creative idea that grows legs and moves in a direction. The direction may be logical or experiential, but it's always fueled by passion and emotion. And if it's based on a universal concept, it can climb onto the silver screen or on top of an entertainment venue filled with stars.

The best ideas for film are visual ideas. They are not ideas of thought from the mind, but rather the physical realm that's filled with action and color. These ideas can be brainstormed or birthed from sketches and playtime. Every successful filmmaker has talked at one time or another about how his idea originated on a paper napkin.

Creativity is one of the most written topics in the world of art, but few books can capture the non-conforming activities that make an artist great. Sure, they can describe think tank processes, impromptu brainstorming activities, or even suggest exercises that stimulate new perspectives. But they can't mentor you in the exhilarating experience birthed between two creative types that drive a positive idea to fruition.

The closest thing to achieving this form of creative reproduction within a workforce is the Disney Imagineers. While I'd highly recommend each of their books, it still won't stir up the creativity within your soul like your own process will.

And there is the rub.

Many creative types feel they need permission to do what it takes to be creative. Or they slap society in the face and do anything that might shock them away from the status quo and into a new light of creation. These extremes are rarely healthy and many times incorporate vices or devices that eventually send the artist into a dark place - some to never return.

It's my personal conviction that developing a movie must be physical. There needs to be pieces of paper all over my walls. My sketchbook needs random thoughts and peculiar ideas plastered all over it. The unrelated elements must be reviewed until a sense of logic is formed.

Forming the related elements into key groupings tend to force a focus that can drive a story forward. By conforming the ideas to fit the needs of the many, new creative perspectives can take hold. After all, no one has ever seen what's been developed on the topic within my mind before. It is truly new and fresh – just like what is in your mind.

The most fascinating thing that develops through this non-specific process is a style that most can see has come from me. No one would be able to conform his or her work to look and feel like the things that I've developed within my mind's eye. It is, therefore, critical that I find people that can help fulfill my dream the way it was birthed within my soul. The collaboration is a must in the world of film, especially since its stories culminate from the fusion of both the arts and sciences.

And, if I were so fortunate as to have the opportunity to create that new story, it would be even more exciting to see it instill certain values to the audience that I support. But my goal is not to teach, as much as it is to entertain. For entertainment, in and of itself, is an excellent tool that helps people catch ideas rather than be taught the same.

It all starts with the simple creation of an idea, which can happen whenever the mood strikes, and, for the professional, whenever he logs time in his calendar. So, take a moment to create something. Pull it out of the air. Or ask a "why" question that hasn't yet been broached. But whatever it is you do, do it in the exact way that you choose, creating your own process.

3X5 Brainstorming Effect

The 3X5 Brainstorming Effect is a tool I created to help students at an art festival take their skills to a new level. The process forces creative thought to expand beyond normal margins of activity. It starts with the premise that the writer has an existing logline that specifies the high concept of the story.

Step One

Review the logline and come up with as many scene ideas as possible. Write each idea on a 3X5 card and stick it randomly on the wall. Do not spend time writing details on the cards, but write enough to jog the memory of the scene created during the brainstorming session.

Step Two

After Step One is exhausted, read the logline again from the viewpoint of an old lady. Again, quickly write each scene idea on a card and randomly post it on the wall.

Step Three

Continue Step Two using different perspectives. Write from the vantage point of a child, prison guard, chimney sweep, etc. Each perspective brings new insights that will culminate into the final story.

Step Four

Review the wall of cards and organize them into logical groupings, patterns or linear thought tracks. Determine which cards support the theme of the story and mark them for plot "B". Determine what cards move the story forward through action and mark them for plot "A".

Step Five

Organize the cards into 8 sequences that tell the best story. Make sure there is a linear flow to the story by adding in transition cards or salting in "B" or "C" plot cards. The "C" plotline is typically for scenes that bring comic relief.

Step Six

Turn each card into a paragraph so it reads like a story. Sit back, relax and read the story to see if it is entertaining, poignant or riveting. Change the paragraphs that don't move the story forward and keep the ones that entice the reader to read the next paragraph. Anything that is great, but doesn't fit the story, put it away for your next project.

These six steps make the building of the first draft's story structure fun and imaginative. It's a fast process that allows the writer to quickly explore an idea to determine if it has enough merit to deserve hundreds of hours developing the story for the silver screen. And it saves a lot of wasted time on those great concepts that don't flesh out.

The Angle of a Story

In talking with numerous filmmakers, preachers and teachers, I've found that all of them have some form of a story to share. They are filled with ideas that will help guide individuals down a recommended path in life and consider things and issues they may have never taken time to address had it not been for their story. But I find one thing perplexing about these master storytellers that most have in common: they typically tell the first version of the story they come up with.

Every valuable story has a right to be shared, but not every perspective on that story will yield the greatest benefit for the viewer or reader. Exploring multiple angles on the same story might open the eyes of its author to key subtleties or nuances that will leverage an emotion or touch a chord in the audiences' lives, empowering them to change.

Playing around with various perspectives or angles on a story takes significant work and shifts the author's perspective from enjoying their own cool story to making sure the audience is directly benefiting from having heard or seen it. It's all about taking the audience on a trip to consider an "argument" that stirs their souls and engages their minds.

Unfortunately, our society is geared toward massive amounts of information, compared to one or two high quality products. An author is forced to make choices that generate a living, over creating a story that changes the way an entire generation thinks. Today, sheer quantity dominates quality.

That's not to say there aren't a few new thoughts out there, but few are releasing products of any consequence.

I've been working on and off, on a feature film script titled "Steele Blue." It started out as an action film because I was in the mood to write some cool action sequences. There was little story involved, as it was an action romp. Then a friend asked me some questions about the characters and as I explained who they were, my friend was fascinated and wanted to know more. I changed the script to bring out those characteristics that were intriguing.

This led to another rewrite, as some of the scenes weren't conducive to drawing out the key points of the characters. It forced me to shift from an action film to the genre of adventure. Once there, the intriguing characters came to life as I alluded to curious facets in their interpersonal relationships.

Another set of rewrites developed as I explored relationships that particularly piqued interest. In doing so, I found the story would be better served as a drama. After choosing to focus more on the heart of one character and explore what her decisions would be in unique circumstances, I shifted the drama to include comedy, adventure and a few thrills.

The story is still the same, but it's told from such a significantly different angle of interest that makes me anxious to see how audiences' react. To whet your appetite a bit, the story is about a maverick detective that hits the streets to protect her teenage son from the drug lord with whom she finds herself falling in love. The key question the action plot raises is whether or not the detective will get her man as a cop, or as a lover.

Had I not explored the various angles on how to tell the story, I would never have discovered the inner conflict the main character faces. It is an intriguing question about the choices one must make. Will she do what *feels* right, or what *is* right, but more difficult? Her dilemma is one that everyone of us face sooner or later. My choice is to explore the new story version and see how it may affect the audiences' future choices.

Taking a look at the same story from different characters or perspectives opens the writer to numerous opportunities to create a story never told before. It also allows the writer to explore life issues that can be handled best indirectly, without offending. Such an approach allows the audience to stretch their thinking and discover new ways to grow as humans, increasing exponentially the story's value.

Five Steps from an Idea to a Script

I attended a special creative writing class at Northwestern University to gain incites from great writers. I had the least amount of writing skills in the room and battled with my emotions. I could sense that by the end of the day, I'd either take advantage of the talent surrounding me to improve my skills or I'd feel bad about my ignorance and give up the craft.

What fascinated me about the class was the incredible word craftsmanship revealed as each writer read his amazing in-class work. However, there was one oddity that surfaced as I read my own lackluster work: it was a story, not a series of polished words with no direction.

My poor ability to wordsmith was obvious, but I soon noticed that I was often the only one that completed the story. Certainly the short time limit was a factor, but I wondered if I was simply more focused on the story than the way in which it was presented. The class' writers were more enthralled with words and their sounds. I was honed in on telling stories that evoked responses.

In one assignment, the instructor told us to write a one-sentence story. It was difficult, but the class members dove into the challenge. When the time came to read our work aloud, everyone else used impressive, polished words – that is everyone, except me. While not as eloquent-sounding as the others', my one-sentence story was complete. In only a few words, I wrote a comedy and was rewarded with the class bursting out in laughter.

As a result, I concluded that most screenwriters either start with their cool ideas or dive into the scenes they can easily visualize, rather than thinking through story structure, themes, and the character development that drive a story.

In fact, most screenwriters follow this pattern:

- An idea pops into the head of an independent screenwriter and he's off to the keyboard, typing at breakneck speed.
- He pulls the paper from the printer and shoves it into his most supportive readers' hands.
- They chug through the 120-page script over a few weeks.
- They finally give feedback about the handful of scenes they loved and point out parts of the story they didn't understand.
- The screenwriter takes another stab at the story and soon finds he added three more scenes that play well, but again, the story is incoherent.

Returning to the keyboard again, he pumps out another 120-pages of a very different version of the story.

- He finds fewer readers available that are willing to give up 3-4 hours of time, but those who work through it find nine loveable scenes, yet still no story.
- After another six months of pleading, looking up old friends and finding new ones to read his work, he sets the unfinished script on the shelf to dive into an entirely new concept that popped into his mind during coffee with an acquaintance.

- This idea is larger than life, and is sure to be a box office success, so he hits the keyboard and starts the process all over again.
- No matter how creative the person is, until he puts the story into a structure that makes sense, he will only have a handful of cool scenes.

To help screenwriters focus on creating a functional story, I've listed the five steps to turn an idea into a script:

Step 1: Logline

Every story worth telling can be reduced to 1 or 2 sentences. This step is incredibly important as you can test your story idea with lots of people in a short time frame without much effort on their part. If they don't like the story, you've lost little time at the keyboard. And, when you've got an idea that piques most people's interest, you have a story blueprint that will help keep your story focused through all writing stages.

Step 2: Step Outline

To create the Step Outline, use a stack of index cards to capture one sentence for each scene in the film. Once the brainstorming of scenes is complete, the cards can be easily moved around a display wall to help determine which scenes you want to use for the inciting incident, various turning points in the plot and the ultimate climax. The cards can be quickly added, changed and moved on the display wall, or tossed into a recycle bin.

Step 3: Pitch

Using this technique, testing the Step Outline with a handful of people is simple and takes only 10 minutes. By reducing the sentences to a couple of pages, you can glance at the display as you share your story pitch with others. This will become critical step in determining what ideas or scenes captured the reviewers' attention, and which ones bored them.

Step 4: Treatment

In Step 4, you will develop each Step Outline sentence into a full paragraph or two. In the Treatment step, create the scenes' subtext by capturing what the characters talk about without using dialogue. And, to better clarify things for Step 5, include in the long form Treatment the characters' thoughts and feelings.

Step 5: First Draft

In Step 5, you transfer the story from the literary world into the visual world. Typically in this step, you include descriptive action, a clear subtext and minimal dialogue. It is also the first time to determine what parts of the story work and flow with the juxtaposition of scenes and pacing.

Professional screenwriters are aware that 60 to 80 percent of what they write during these steps will not survive in the final screenplay, but they know that they need the process to create great story.

Anyone can write a story, but few will persevere to develop a *great* story.

Elements of a Great Pitch

I had a unique off-the-cuff opportunity to successfully pitch a story concept to a producer. He was excited about the project based on how I shared the story and told me to contact my attorney to close our deal.

A few days later, I had a writer pitch me a story concept in hopes of getting me to collaborate on her screenplay, but her pitch left me without any desire to read her script. The project died before it could be launched, all because she didn't understand the key elements in a pitch.

Pitching a story requires three key elements:

1. A unique idea or concept.
2. A marketable story.
3. Great story telling.

The unique idea is very difficult to accomplish in this day and age when studio marketers want something familiar, but different. They immediately reject the same ole thing, as well as the totally new thing. In order to know how to sell the project, studio marketers are attracted to familiar concepts with a slight twist to interest a potential audience.

A marketable story must be relevant and cutting edge. It should be visual, yet touching. It must satisfy niche markets, while being universal enough to reach the masses. It has to appeal to what the market manager might be thinking at the time, or you must convince him your story will set a new trend in motion.

If by some chance you master the first two abilities, the story is the last thing that will make or break your pitch.

For great project pitches, always:

Create a Connection

People want to work with great relationships that are built by "people persons." The energy that comes from a positive collaborator is essential to your story's success. The pitch session is the time and place to be the person your friends like, not the cold business person you may need to be during negotiations.

Showing a sincere interest in the person you're meeting with will go a long way, especially if you take the time to listen to what he has to say about your story. All too often, a writer is so preoccupied with telling his story that he doesn't notice that making a simple tweak could be the very thing that lands him a deal.

In other words, get the prospect to want to do business with you, but be real in the process. Phonies are easily spotted in Hollywood.

Share with Charismatic Magnetism

Next, share your story as if you are consumed by it. Help the prospect to visualize scenes as you talk about them. Tell the story dramatically when you're at an intense point in your story. Make the tale humorous when you share the comedic bits. Be an entertainer in the presentation, and see if you aren't paid with applause and a contract.

Set Up the Story

Tell the producer what makes your story great. Explain when and how you came up with the story, as the heart behind your story will add to its value. In fact, if you can share the genesis of your story, while showing how it's grounded in reality, you will surely grab his attention. And no matter what, make sure he understands why altogether the story is relevant to the world about you.

Introduce Your Characters

Share enough about your characters so the producer gets a feel for who those characters are. Cause him to become emotionally engaged with them and learn how to care about them. Then, turn up the story with plenty of jeopardy so he needs to hear every bit of your story in order to be satisfied.

Get Real and Relaxed

These key elements will make your pitch session a success. However, one simple caution: Don't indicate that you're uncomfortable when making the presentation. Of course you'll naturally be nervous, so make sure you take enough time to get to know everyone in the room and help them to become familiar with you before you begin.

Being real and relaxed are still the two greatest tools you have on your side. Producers and studio executives deal with fake all day and crave those real, down-to-earth conversations and stories. So, just be yourself and have fun telling the story you know all too well.

12 Steps in Crafting A Treatment that Sells

Treatments were once a tool for the writer to work out the concepts and beats of the story before spending weeks writing a screenplay. This saved time and made story and beat rewrites easier. It also allowed the writer to improve or tweak the story after meeting with producers, directors or key actors.

Today treatments are a tool to sell the story and often writers create several versions to facilitate different meetings. For instance, a studio executive doesn't have time to read more than a paragraph or possibly a single page, while a producer may prefer the three-pager, while a director the 20-pager. A writer might even craft a 40+ pager for structural work before diving into the screenplay.

Regardless of the need for varying lengths, there are 12 steps needed in creating a treatment:

1. Keep it brief

Move the story quickly, with concise wording. Use common terms while clarifying key story elements. Highlight the plot and avoid unnecessary details.

2. Show and Tell

Treatments must make it easy for the reader to "see" the story visually in his or her mind. Stimulate the reader's emotions, with the right pacing and word choice.

3. Test the Pitch

Sharing the story with friends is the best way to test the concept, visualization and emotional response of the listener or reader. This will allow the writer to tweak whatever parts of the story tend to lull and give him or her permission to drop those beloved scenes that just don't work.

4. Appeal with Visuals

The best treatment looks and reads as easily as a short story written in narrative form. Construct with occasional quotation marks for dialogue, and avoid mentioning any film terms or technical screenplay structure.

5. Stimulate with Drama and Emotion

The treatment story should be saturated with active, three-dimensional characters using focused dialogue - all designed to quickly progress the story. Detail should be limited and should not slow down the read.

6. Use the Present Tense

The treatment must use present tense to place the reader in the scene as it happens, just like in the movies. Action verbs will enhance this sense of immediacy.

7. Hook and Tease

Hook the reader's interest by making the story's subject uniquely different than anything else seen. Tease the reader by raising questions in the reader's mind, compelling them to seek the answers and finish the read.

8. Reveal Key Characters

The treatment should cause the reader to understand the story's main characters, their attitudes and how the protagonist changes throughout the story. Also, the reader should bond with the main character, so the treatment should provide a "Save the Cat" moment early on.

9. Clear Scene Structure

The structure of the paragraphs and the description of the settings must be in keeping with the style of the show as well as clarify scene and act breaks. The treatment should be concise enough to not slow down the reader's experience.

10. Include Key Scenes Only

The obligatory through-line scenes are important to include in the treatment along with enough of the B-storyline to clarify the story's theme. Plots C, D, or E are not typically addressed unless they overlap with the action plotline. For brevity, not all scenes from the action plotline should be included.

11. Remember those Turning Points

All turning points, cliffhangers, and other twists in the plot must be included in the treatment. This is critical, because each one propels the reader into the next act or scene and may send the main character in a new direction.

12. Follow Media Treatment Rules

Prescribed treatment formats in the film and television industry should be used as required. However, there is one thing that nullifies this recommendation: A treatment is great because its writer is an expert dramatist, which overrides everything else. Just focus on entertaining the reader at all costs.

The typical treatment length for a Movie of the Week is seven to 15 pages long, broken into seven or eight acts, depending on the television network. The length of a feature film treatment is 10-20 pages and separated into three acts. However, other lengths will be required for various meetings.

Three Key Factors in Optioning Story Rights

During the first quarter of every year, I review numerous books and consider optioning them to be made into a feature film. It doesn't matter how many books I go after, the end result is usually the same. There is a 25% chance I will obtain the "right to option" the story, a 5% chance I will actually option it, and a 2% chance I will buy the rights.

There are three key factors I face in optioning story rights. Each one of those factors has to work out perfectly in order to obtain the rights and create the screenplay. To succeed, I've found that I have to educate the author, agree on a contract, and change my approach to suit the author.

Educate the Author

The first step in obtaining the rights is to educate the author on the differences between media. Seldom do audiences say that the movie was just like the book. Most people either like the book and hate the movie, or like the movie and hate the book, unless both were just okay.

What makes for a great literary piece is almost the exact opposite of what makes for a great visual piece. The only thing the media has in common is their attempts to sway the audience's emotions, albeit by different techniques.

In the literary world the author can help the audience get into the mind of the characters. That wouldn't work as well in film, as the entire movie would be interrupted by narration. These disruptions would pull the viewer out of the story or remind them that they are watching a movie, rather than experiencing the circumstances with the character.

A good book can take the audience on a journey or exploration that they help create with their imagination. In film, the director uses his imagination to select the specifics of the journey and invites the audience to view what he has already explored.

Most great books fail on the screen, while mediocre ones succeed. This is due to great books having its main plot line filled with heady thought, emotions and character bonding. Film on the other hand, typically moves the emotional components of the story to the B-plotline.

Many times great books require its B-plotline to be elevated in a movie as an action plotline in order for it to succeed. The opposite is also true; books that don't connect well with the reader typically are driven by action, which translates well to the screen.

Agree on a Contract

There are three phases in most agreements. Each phase requires an outlay of cash or percentage of the film. These phases are highly negotiable and require a tremendous amount of diplomacy to achieve, as it involves two artists from two very different media.

The three phases include: the right to option, the option, and the purchasing of the story rights including copyright transfer. The phased agreement typically carries three signature sections for the execution of each part.

The right to option the story gives the purchaser time to develop the story for the screen. It may or may not be a successful attempt based on the huge differences in media. This part is filled with a lot of risk for the writer, director or producer who is attempting to obtain the rights. A treatment is typically written during this phase to help the creative team understand how the film would play out.

The option typically kicks in once the purchaser knows the story will translate. While there is no guarantee that it will, he has found at least a handful of nuggets that will help the process and make the next phase of development worth the risk. He writes the first draft of the screenplay, creates a synopsis and forms a pitch in order to shop the story with potential investors, talent and distributors.

The screenwriter purchases the book's rights once there is an agreement signed for a big name talent, financing or distribution. While this doesn't guarantee the story is ever produced, the book's author -- depending on the contract -- can take a good amount of money to the bank.

Since the negotiations are very people- and needs- focused, everything I shared might be completely different between agreements. For instance, some producers prefer to jump straight into the option and skip the first phase, while other producers might want to hire a writer during the first phase rather than wait for the second.

The bigger or the less risk adverse production companies usually buy the rights outright, sometimes just to keep it away from the competition, and set it on the shelf for the contract's duration. Moderate-sized production companies buy the option up front so they can move quickly with their existing partners in finance and distribution. Smaller, niche, or boutique production companies include the right to option the story because it drops their risk down to something palatable, knowing that few literary stories translate well to the screen.

Comic books translate particularly well to the screen because of their visual inception. The mind of the author translated during the story's formation and produced visuals playing the main role.

Change Approach to Suit the Author

I've worked with humble writers and I've worked with prima donnas. Some have been fearful that their perfect story would be slightly altered and others could care less about major changes. There are writers who believe their own press and think they are God's gift to the film world, while others are surprised their story rights are desired.

The controller types are the most difficult with which to work. One of my friends had a book deal that progressed well until the author stepped in -- which his contract allowed -- and demanded thousands of dollars in changes. That development blew the film's budget, causing it to never be released.

My first book deal involved an unattached and angry author. The story suffered because we couldn't ask him key clarifying questions for fear he'd file another lawsuit to change the contract. The film failed miserably in the United States, but thankfully, it was a huge success overseas. There we broke even.

There is a fine balance between an author controlling a film's production to its detriment and the author being engaged to support her story. The ideal is one who is on standby to answer specific questions without rambling on to other ideas, and is willing to trust the creative production team with what they do best. Unfortunately, those types of authors are hard to find.

The hands-off authors are typically so far distant you can't ask them clarifying questions without getting them more engaged. However, once engaged, they become a train wreck that demands a lot of time- and energy-consuming interaction. Those that start off engaged and/or demanding constantly force the creative team to insulate themselves. It the relationship continues unchecked, the production team might change the story just to flaunt their own creative rights.

The worst part isn't how the author behaves, but rather how the purchaser behaves. I've found myself in many situations where I wanted to, but thankfully didn't, make a bad decision to put an author in his place, or purchase a story that I couldn't translate, just because of the good or bad relationship existing between the author and me.

I made a big mistake with one children's title when I kept the author's favorite scene in the movie. My expertise told me to trash it, but I kept it because of the relationship I had built with the author. As expected, the critics panned the movie with every article referencing that scene which just didn't fit the film. The only thing that made it worse was listening to the author rant on and on about the scene.

The bottom line is that there are no rules to follow concerning the various types of deals made with authors. However, educating the author, agreeing on a contract and finding the best ways to communicate heart and soul will always be a part of transitioning a book to a film, regardless of the cutting edge deal being discussed.

Getting a Book Optioned

There are authors who have created a lot of great stories, but are still waiting to see their books morph into movies. This is due in part to the Hollywood standards used to determine what stories translate well to the film screen. Many never get that far because of the dread they experience releasing their titles to be reworked into film formats. Often those transitions include dramatic changes in style, content or theme.

However, most authors willing to allow a trusted production team to alter their stories may have no idea how to get their book into the hands of right companies. The secret to finding the right production company is simply hard, diligent research.

A quick dive into production company research provides a list of thousands of possible companies. As of this writing, there are six big studio production companies. Independents make up the rest, including 242 in Chicago, Illinois and 66 in Seattle, Washington. There are 516 companies labeled "Christian," and on the various lists go, not including companies launched with the sole purpose of making and releasing one specific motion picture.

After finding potential production companies, certain filtering systems will lead to the right companies for a particular story. The following 10 parts should be incorporated if a book is under consideration:

1. Proactive Hero

The story's main character or protagonist must be active. He must be motivated and decisive, rather than passive. The character must grow throughout his journey and overcome whatever restrained him in the story's opening.

2. Universal Story

The story must be based on an high concept and understandable by the average person. It should be based on common experiences, but from a unique viewpoint. The story needs to be able to capture the attention of the audience, regardless of their interests in the story's issues.

3. Flawed Protagonist

The main character must be flawed in a way that reveals elements of the human condition to which others can relate. The character must face struggles through which he must battle to achieve his goals. By the end of the story, he should be able to figure out a way to turn his flaw into strength or a tool he'll use to save the day or accomplish his mission.

4. Great Action Plotline

The story must move forward through physical action or life-changing decisions. This movement must be strong enough to carry the reader through every aspect of the story. A great action plot is understandable with the audio muffled or dialogue deleted.

5. Story With 7-8 Set Pieces

Set pieces are those iconic scenes designed to have an obvious imposing effect on the audience. They are the scenes in a film ideal for trailers, that stand out and convey the film's uniqueness. These types of scenes create buzz and drive people to pay good money to see the movie. Rarely are films made, let alone promoted, without these notable moments purposely embedded into their story lines.

6. Structure Using 3, 7 Or 8 Acts

Most Hollywood films use the three-act structure, but Movies of the Week (MOWs) are further broken down into 7 or 8 acts, depending on the network -- the difference being in the structure of the first act. If the story is not able to fit this structure, it won't be purchased or if the network purchases it, they will significantly change the stories to fit their production patterns.

7. Visual Storyline

Motion pictures are designed for movement. While that sounds ridiculously obvious, there are many people who want their talking head story to be on the silver screen. If the story is dialogue driven, then the producers should consider radio or theatre. If the story is thought-driven, it is better off staying as a book. But, if the story has action, movement or some semblance of motion, it should work on the big screen. A film's storyline must be filled with visual action.

8. Raise An Overarching Question

Questions must be raised in audiences' minds to maintain their attention and drive their desire for the next scene. If the story has numerous scene-by-scene questions answered throughout the main character's journey with an overarching question that isn't answered until the climax, then the story is ideal for film.

9. Entertainment Value

Audiences flock to the theater to have fun, laugh, cry, be frightened or stimulated, as well as other emotional responses to entertainment. Books with tragedy or comedy that draw upon emotions and are truly entertaining have a better shot at being made into films.

10. Professional Author

The author needs to be audience-minded and professional in his approach to a film project. An author, who is more concerned about his content than the audience, would not be a good fit. The option agreement is a business proposition that takes a story and translates it to a completely different medium. It is not a personal agreement that takes someone's baby away from them and raises it to be something they didn't want it to be. If the author can't understand that difference, then movies are not for him.

Those authors that fit all ten of the above criteria will find their stories selling for top dollar. Some authors, with a large number of the above items matching their books, will get a lot of requests, but might not ever see their books made into movies.

And, other authors will never be asked because their stories so definitely failed to match the 10-point criteria.

I remember meeting one author whose writing was perfectly situated to receive numerous options. Since none of his stories were produced, he got wise and raised his upfront fees, knowing his back end fees were of little value. He told me that he made six figures a year from selling options and no longer cared if any of his stories ever became movies.

Most authors never see six figures because independent companies develop the majority of options. In fact, authors usually laugh at the size of their royalty checks. However, the authors are very excited at the huge jump in book sales created by the movie. I've known authors whose book sales doubled with a film release. Others' sales jumped by ten to twenty times after their books turned into film projects.

One author sold around 40,000 units a year and after her movie released, sales jumped to 150,000 a year. The notoriety she received from the film caused her next title to sell 350,000 units in the first six months, without a film deal. Another author sold 10,000 books a year and his film deal shot book sales up to over one million copies in 18 months.

Option agreements are valuable to many authors. However, some prefer trying to write the screenplays themselves and find soon after they lack the mastery of the craft needed to generate sales. Most screenwriters write numerous screenplays for years before their skill level hits a place of value for production companies to consider.

Authors eventually learn that book writing uses a significantly different set of skills, which leaves them working for years trying to develop the new techniques. Other authors realize that their core abilities are in writing novels and choose to leave screenwriting to the experienced.

The Beat Sheet

Box office hits like Star Trek use "beats" to grab the audiences' attention and bring structure to the storyline. Most cinematic stories have 40 – 45 beats and are distributed within the 45 – 60 scenes it takes to tell a 110-page story. Larger cinematic action and adventure films are quicker paced and distribute the key beats over 120 – 140 scenes within 120 story pages.

For this chapter, the page counts listed are based on a 110-page script.

While the pacing and average duration changes between genres and directing styles, the main backbone of the story structure consists of 16 – 18 beats. The below 16 beats are standard in the industry:

ACT 1: The Set-up

- Opening Imagery
- Bonding Hero to Audience
- Statement of Theme
- The Catalyst
- Gulp, Here Goes
- Turning Point 1

ACT 2: Development

- Intro Sub-Plot B
- One Sheet Pay-off
- Mid-Point & Raising the Stakes
- Empower the Antagonist

- Lost Hope
- The Inner Battle
- Turning Point 2

ACT 3: Finale

- Battle for Success
- Climax
- Closing Imagery

Act 1: The Set-up

Opening Imagery

An opening scene sets a movie's genre, tone, pace and mood. It typically gives the audience a chance to see the hero before he becomes the hero.

In Star Trek, we see Kirk's dad in a sacrificial battle where he heroically saves thousands of people including his newborn, Kirk. The sequence set the tone for the story and introduced Kirk as a person of great heroic potential.

Bonding Hero to Audience

In the first five minutes of a script, screenwriters bond the audience with the hero using comedy, coolness or crisis. The key is to have the audience experience the unique moment with the hero.

In his teen years, Kirk stole his uncle's car and turned it into a joyride, which demonstrated his sense of adventure. While his acting out was to avoid his heroic potential, he took an adventurous risk by jumping from the car just before it zoomed off the cliff and fell into the rocky canyon.

Statement of Theme

The film's theme is revealed in the first five minutes. Typically, a character poses a thought-provoking question to the hero. Many screenwriters use this moment to introduce the Central Question that drives the Action Plot.

In Star Trek, Kirk and Spock shared the role of the protagonist. Spock drove the theme and Kirk the action plot. Spock's father introduced the theme with young Spock, "You are capable of determining your own destiny, the question is, which path will you choose?"

The Catalyst

Around pages 10 to 12, the story moves into motion and sends the audience into the adventure. This can be done with a letter or mysterious package arriving, someone dying, or the arrival of unique news with a deadline.

In Star Trek, Captain Pike challenged Kirk, "Your father was captain of a starship for 12 minutes...he saved 800 lives. Including yours. I dare you to do better. Enlist in Starfleet."

Gulp, Here Goes

Between pages 12 and 24 the hero debates the "Should I, or Shouldn't I?" by verbalizing his thoughts. Then he gulps hard and takes action.

For Kirk, his point of decision took place on his motorcycle, watching workers build the Enterprise. He imagined his future and debated within his heart whether or not he should join Starfleet.

Turning Point 1

This scene introduces a turn of events that forces the hero out of the thesis world and into an upside down version or its antithesis. It sends the hero in a new direction, which gives him the skills needed to succeed back in the thesis world and resolve the story. The scene takes place around pages 17 to 21.

Cadet Kirk is suspended from Starfleet duty until his hearing concludes from his alleged cheating on a test. With all other students being sent early into active duty to determine the extent of an anomaly in space, Dr. McCoy gives Kirk a drug that requires emergency treatment on board the Enterprise.

Act 2: Development

Intro Sub-Plot B

By page 30, the audience needs a little break from the Action Plotline, an ideal time to introduce an underlying internal heart-based story. It's also the time to introduce new characters that live in the upside-down world into which the story turned. The strongest characters would be the antithesis of characters introduced in Act 1.

Since Star Trek had duel protagonists, Spock was the person with the love interest. During this portion of the film, ensemble characters were introduced.

One Sheet Pay-off

During pages 30 through 55, the screenwriter delivers the expected goods promised to the audience in the One Sheet (movie poster) or trailer. During these scenes, the hero learns what he needs for Act 3, embraces it and eventually lives it. The hero's education is often accomplished through fun and games.

Kirk and Sulu do a free fall from space into the atmosphere to save the planet Vulcan from destruction. Sulu battles with a sabre and Kirk uses hand-to-hand combat.

Raising the Stakes

Page 55 is the top of the story's arc. This scene typically provides the hero a false hope, where he seems to get everything he thinks he wants. He believes life can't get much better and finds he has a lot to lose in the coming pages. The fun actions end as the pace picks up as the story races toward the finale. Raising the stakes, he is set up for Turning Point 2, which is the antithesis of this scene.

Since Kirk and Spock's relationship is one of the strongest elements in Star Trek, putting their relationship in jeopardy escalates the story for the audience.

Empower the Antagonist

During pages 55 to 75, the hero's hope is dashed as the bad guys move in and their evil increases. This is where chase scenes occur, bad guys regroup and the antagonist focuses efforts on destroying the hero. It is the antithesis of the One Sheet Pay-Off scenes. The larger the evil one becomes, the more powerful the story's climax.

In Star Trek, Nero corned the Enterprise and put the entire crew at risk. He also stated his personal vendetta for Spock and made him watch the destruction of his own planet.

Lost Hope

By page 75, the hero has lost hope. The bad guys have the upper hand and the hero sits in self-pity. This moment is the antithesis of "Raising the Stakes" on page 55.

Spock ordered Kirk off of the ship and marooned him on a snowy ice planet, creating despair and lost hope within Kirk.

The Inner Battle

The hero explores his feelings of darkness within his own soul during the next 3-5 minutes, on pages 80 to 85). He questions why everyone has forsaken him.

In Star Trek, Kirk made the difficult decision to risk his life for the crew of the Enterprise.

Turning Point 2

This Turning Point is launched when the light bulb goes on and the hero realizes how to solve the problems in the Action Plot and Sub-Plot B. It merges the external story with the internal heart-based story and creates a solution for the hero to apply.

Kirk made Spock burst out with rage and stand down from duty, leaving the captain spot open. Kirk took the captain's chair and its responsibilities.

Act 3: Finale

Battle for Success

Pages 85 to 105 bring resolution to the Action Plot and Sub-Plot B. The hero uses the lessons learned in Act 2 to destroy the bad guys, turn over the old world 's way of thinking in Act 1 and launch the new world's way of thinking in an emotionally satisfying way with a clear directive and future.

Kirk and Spock joined forces to battle Nero and his crew.

Climax

Around page 105, the story line provides the audience with the ultimate emotional moment as the hero claims victory. If it doesn't feel climatic, the story wasn't properly set up in Act 1 or the story died in Act 2. If the emotions aren't significantly raised, the bad guys weren't empowered enough in Act 2.

Kirk and Spock destroyed Nero and the red matter with a twist that amazed the audience.

Closing Imagery

The epilogue happens between pages 105 and 110 and proves that the new world's ways of thinking are real, accepted and beneficial to all. It is the antithesis of the Opening Imagery.

Thanks to the Enterprise, the United Federation of Planets maintains the good life for its people and Kirk receives his official command and is awarded for the success of the mission.

Caution should be exercised in following this beat sheet, as many stories tend to create its own beats and pacing. Finding the story's internal pulse will help the screenwriter stay focused on the message and emotional appeal.

Additional beats will be added if the story requires a Sub-Plot C, D, or E.

Creating the Hero: A Look at Avatar

The most successful stories are those where the main character becomes the hero by the climax of the film. The hero walks through a path of change and growth that the audience can follow. The process itself creates a bond between the character and the audience, which develops into emotional support through the second act and emerges with some form of the audience cheering on the rising hero by the film's climax.

Avatar's simple hero story structure was key in integrating the incredible effects and new technologies into a motion picture worthy of $2.78B (at the time this chapter was written) in box office receipts. Due to its huge success, I thought I'd review the hero portion of the film's story structure.

Normal Mundane Life

The hero starts out as a non-hero that lives a straightforward innocent life. He lives in a mundane world where he functions in a typical fashion that might make the average person yawn. This soon-to-be hero has a desire to be or experience something more, but continues to live his mundane day-to-day life.

In Avatar, the main character Jake lives a non-adventurous life due to a spinal injury that restricts him to a wheel chair. His legs were well atrophied, yet the desire of his heart was for adventure.

Toss in a Catalyst

Before the audience gets too turned off by the non-hero's life, the writer adds a catalyst to the mix. This ingredient can come in many forms, but it always pushes the hero into an extraordinary adventure. It breaks the mold of the mundane and sets the hero on a path that will continue to escalate until the climax.

Jake learns that his identical twin brother Tommy, who was set to be an avatar user, was murdered for the paper in his wallet. Since avatars are based on exact DNA matches, Tommy's avatar becomes available for use by Jake.

Reveals His Hesitation

Many films die during the second act because the audience doesn't understand the growth the hero must accomplish in order to face his adversary in Act Three. To set up the contrast in Act One, the writer reveals the hero's uncertainties, fears, or any other form of reluctance that could hold him back.

Jake finds himself in a terrifying set of circumstances during his first visit to the rainforest. He encounters many new and weird creatures, but all fear breaks loose when he finds himself in between a six-legged Hammerhead Titanothere and a Thanator with an ear splitting roar. Within a few minutes, Jake realizes that he is not cut out for the adventure and wants out.

Introduce the Mentor

The Archetype or hero's mentor is introduced to share a few wise words, give perspective or a little nudge to get the hero moving into the adventure. The initial movement sends the hero into a sort of training that develops what he will need to win or overcome by the climax of the film.

In Avatar, this role is split up between Grace and Neytiri. Grace helps Jake to appreciate the scientific perspective on the Na'vi culture and Neytiri teaches him the ways of her people.

Turning Point Sends Hero into Obstacles

At the end of Act One, the hero is catapulted into Act Two through a twist in the plot that sends him in a new and unexpected direction from his goals. Jake finds himself in a new world that is the antithesis of his mundane world. This transition kicks off the hero's transformation into what he needs to become in order to fight the eminent battle in act three.

Jake is captured by the Na'vi and is brought to Mo'at, who wants to observe him. She determines that Neytiri will train him in their ways. Colonel Quaritch agrees to Jake participating in the program in hopes of learning how to control the natives. Jake finds himself with numerous obstacles to overcome in learning how to live like a Na'vi.

Plagued by Obstacles

The hero is inundated by a series of obstacles that get worse with each mini-victory, forcing the hero to step up to another level, eventually bringing him to a place of confidence with the higher skills needed for the final battle just before the climax.

Jake must learn archery, tracking, riding, language skills and how to bond and tame a banshee. He must fulfill the Na'vi warrior's required right of passage, which is bonding with a banshee and becoming an Ikran Makto (One who rides mountain banshees).

A Night of Despair

The obstacles rise to the point where the hero faces a dark night of the soul and desires to give up because all hope seems lost.

By the time Jake's love interest grows with Neytiri and he has been accepted into the tribe after accomplishing his right of passage, he plays a unique role that brings death and destruction to the people he learned to love. He loses everything and is no longer welcome among the humans or the Na'vi.

Resurrected Hope

Avatar's Third Act kicks off with a redemptive moment, as the hero's soul rises to the ultimate challenge. He decides to step up to seize the moment and capture the prize. He enters battle with a cheering audience spurring him on.

Jake turns to Grace and his other human friends to help him get back to the Na'vi in his Avatar. They mobilize the chambers and take one up into the heights where radio signals and tracking devices won't work. Jake gets another chance and warns the Na'vi of the pending battle. To get their attention, Jake realizes that he will have to do something that only a few Na'vi had ever attempted throughout history: capturing and bonding with the Leonopteryx, the king of the mountain banshees.

The Enemy Rises

The moment the hero's enemy realizes that he is stepping up, the chase begins and the enemy sets out to destroy the hero in an all-out battle.

Colonel Quaritch deems Jake a traitor and orders an attack on the Na'vi and their sacred grounds.

The Hero Wins

The hero uses all he learned in Act Two to overcome the enemy and win the prize. The enemy is destroyed or sent away until the sequel and the hero returns home to his once mundane, but no longer frustrated, life. He is now a full-fledged hero.

Jake leads the army of the Na'vi and several other clans into battle against the humans. He uses his knowledge of both cultures and tools to win the battle.

Developing Paradoxical Characters

Making a character interesting drives the audience's desire to follow his or her goals and outcomes. The audience wants to get behind a character and cheer him on, but they must first be drawn to him in a unique way that inspires exploration of the character. This is best accomplished by using a paradox within the character's life or personality.

The television and film phenomenon titled "M.A.S.H." was known for it's paradoxical characters. Alan Alda's Korean Conflict-immersed character of Hawkeye was diametrically opposed to war and wanted no part of it, yet every time he desired to go AWOL, the loudspeaker would announce the in coming wounded and stop him in his tracks. Hawkeye was drawn to the operating room because saving lives was more important than his hatred of war.

These two opposing drivers made the Hawkeye character enjoyable to watch and raised numerous questions in the minds of the audience. They needed to understand what made him tick. During its eleven seasons, people came to love Hawkeye even though they never knew what to expect next, even though his consistency was amazing.

The best way to develop an interesting character is by starting with his flaw. This flaw will have a visible action associated with it to play well on screen. To add strength to the character, it's important to never explain the flaw, but just demonstrate it. The actions should be divided up into three distinct visuals.

What the flaw causes him to do in:

1. Public.

2. A small group of friends.

3. Private.

Once the flaw is notably in place, the dialogue can create further conflict or raise additional questions with the audience. The visuals will help connect the various demonstrated flaw elements to the character in a way that the audience can understand. This makes change or growth in the character at a later point in the story is much easier, as all you have to do is change the visual – cluing in the audience that he has changed his ways.

The best way to express the paradox throughout the show is to take the flaw and determine what it might look like as a blessing. For instance, the person that can be stubborn can also persevere. Perseverance can look very similar to stubbornness, but with a positive spin.

For example, Hawkeye hated war because too many people died, yet being a surgeon prevented him from abandoning the conflict because in his mind, if he left, many more would die.

The paradox within Hawkeye's character was based on that crucial flaw, and was developed throughout the series. It was his Achilles' heel or the basis of his human condition – the very part of Hawkeye with which we all intimately identified and sympathized.

Creating a person that is overall good and simply gets better by the end of the film does nothing for the audience. It's only when we see and understand their humanity and flaws that we can relate and then cheer them on into a better, more mature life. We love rags to riches stories, not rich to filthy rich stories. In this case, I'm speaking of the richness of their character development, but we would find the same to hold equally true about financial wealth.

So, try writing a flawed character that you can turn into an overcomer. Create that person who can turn his or her negative characteristic into a positive one. Turn that obnoxious, stubborn person into one that perseveres long enough for help to arrive after an airplane goes down on a deserted island.

Or, maybe you want that shy person to be the only one that listens well enough to figure out the answer that spares a man's life in the eleventh hour. Or, perhaps you can save the day by writing about a scrawny kid that is constantly ridiculed until the day he is locked in a closet of a burning house. And without effort, he becomes the only one to make it through the vent to get help and unlock the door to free the others seconds before affixation.

Finding that all-important paradox provides the audience plenty of entertainment and allows the writer unlimited creativity to discover the resolution. It also sets up a great form of character development that every serious screenwriter should embrace. It also provides a character that can provide substantial irony for audiences' entertainment.

Developing a 4D Character

It's easy to develop a single-sided character, by saying he's a maverick or any other stereotypical label like "thief," "Boy Scout," or "law student." Using a well-known label allows you to dive directly into your plot, requiring less screen time to develop the main character. However, using stereotypes hinders you from making a character-driven film.

Developing a paradox within the character gives you leverage to expand the single story into multiple sequels or a series. Adding in the opposite characteristic under certain circumstances develops the paradox and a far more interesting character.

Pierce in M.A.S.H. was such a character. He hated war, but could never leave a wounded person behind. Every time he was due to leave, another chopper filled with the wounded was inbound, forcing him to override his hate of war with his compassion for the wounded. His conscience wouldn't allow him to walk away from a wounded person, no matter how passionately he wanted to leave the war zone.

Adding a third dimension to a character, based on an internal secret that the audience doesn't know, develops a greater emotional range and a far more realistic character. Many actors develop this angle within their own character to create realism, so it would be only natural for the screenwriter to supply it. The story angle could be absurd or devastating, but it should be something the main character would never share. An example might be the main character having been raped by his drunk, abusive mother who never remembered the incident once she sobered.

The fourth dimension requires a reality factor that is birthed from within the main character's surroundings. This is the opposite of the standard process of creating supporting characters that slowly reveal certain truths about the main character as the show progresses. While all the standard books will tell you the reveals must come from the other characters -- which is why they are called "supporting" characters -- the 4D process requires the main character to adjust his thoughts and actions, based on with whom he interacts.

This new 4D process was developed to reflect the real life scenarios of how people ebb and flow in conversation with the people or person they are currently communicating with through dialogue. Some of these elements naturally happen as a screenwriter writes conflict into the dialog. When planned out, the main character can be even more interesting and complex.

For this system to work properly, the main character has to adjust his comments and actions based on those around him or those that are absent. The best way to explore this dimension is by asking the questions below.

Whatever it is that he does, how does it make him act or respond:

When he is alone?

When he is with another person?

When he is in a group?

Once you have this fourth element in place and you're able to demonstrate it under one of the above circumstances numerous times throughout the film, you can then break the habit of him doing the action to instantly reveal that he has changed or grown.

This tool works best in showing how the character eventually grows to overcome his circumstances or the story's antagonist. The more subtle the demonstrated change, the more realistic the character and the story. These simple steps make it simple to create a compelling complex 4D character worth watching.

Transforming A Character

In the screenplay ***Tried & True***, written by Guy Cote and me, the film opens with the protagonist or hero being trapped in a form of slavery that is perceived as freedom. By the end of the film, he had become his own free man. To move him from slavery in Act 1 to freedom in Act 3, we had to take him through several developmental stages within two hours of screen time.

I used the ABCs & D of transformation to make sure my character arrived emotionally at the right place by the climax of the film. The below steps make use of this chart:

START A B C D END

Step One

Determine the positive trait you want for the protagonist by the end of the film. Write that trait down under letter A. For our story I wrote "Freedom."

Step Two

Determine the opposite or the contradiction of that trait, and write it down under letter C. There I wrote, "Slavery."

Step Three

Determine what is half way between A and C and write the word down under B. I wrote, "Restraint."

Step Four

Determine what the double negative of C is and write it down under D. I wrote, "Slavery perceived as Freedom". This is the double negative because nothing is worse than being a slave, except for being one without knowing it. Then again, self-enslavement might be worse.

Step Five

Align the ABCs & D in reverse order of the story.

ACT 1	ACT 2A	ACT 2B	ACT 3
D	C	B	A

Step Six

Write the character development traits into the story. Since each act is about 25 pages, you can spread out your development of each condition within the 25 pages. The idea is to take the character from their worst state to their best state in 25 page increments.

My character went from:

ACT 1	ACT 2A	ACT 2B	ACT 3
Slavery Perceived as Freedom	Slavery	Restraint	Freedom

In Act 1 of ***Tried & True***, the Hero is a man who enjoys women and drinks. It is his choice lifestyle because it is the opposite of what his father does, or so he thinks. What he doesn't realize is that the lifestyle controls him.

In Act 2A the Hero finds himself struggling to solve his problems and finds that he is drawn or hooked, like a slave, to women and drinks for a quick temporary fix, but is redirected by the Heroine of the story, which helps his character to grow.

In Act 2B, the Hero doesn't need anyone's help to realize that women and drinks don't solve his problem and he decides to restrain himself from returning to that path.

By Act 3, the Hero becomes a new man that faces his struggles head on and no longer craves women nor drinks. In his freedom, the Hero finds true love and happiness.

Movies Told in Eight Sequences

When a painter wants to capture an image on canvas from a photograph, he typically will divide the picture into quadrants in order to focus on the detail and maintain proper proportions. Filmmakers do something similar by dividing their story into eight sections.

The question most often asked is "Why eight?" when the story is based on a three-act structure. The answer comes from history. In the early days of the cinema, 20-minute reels were delivered to theaters with about 15 minutes worth of film on each reel. When the reel was played, a little dot in the top right corner of the film would appear toward the end of the reel to notify the projectionist it was time to switch to the next reel on a second projector, giving the audience a seamless uninterrupted movie.

The camera manufacturers built their equipment with 20-minute reels knowing the cinematographer would get about 15 minutes of story out of each reel. When television came along, the 15-minute standard was adopted and videotape was designed for about 15 minutes of programming on a 20-minute reel or cassette.

Directors and editors found themselves constantly working in 15-minute increments in order to tell their story, so they quickly adapted to the standard and learned how to tell stories incrementally through a series of sequences. Even television directors got on the bandwagon and tried to heighten the last scene on every reel to keep the audience riveted in hopes that they would continue watching after the commercials.

The typical 2-hour movie is therefore made up of 8 sections of 15 minutes each. Since dramatic screenplays are written in a way that one page equates to about one minute of screen time, the average 2-hour movie is 110 pages in length. There is also an average of one scene per minute of screen time, which gives the screenwriter 12-15 scenes per sequence in order to tell the action plotline. A mixture of shorter scenes and sequences gives enough room to salt in an additional subplot or two.

Act 1 is comprised of two sequences. Act 2 is divided at the midpoint creating two sequences in Act 2A and two sequences in Act 2B. And, Act 3 is also made up of two sequences. In between each Act is a turning point that sends the main character in a different direction than expected, which catapults the viewer into the next segment of the story.

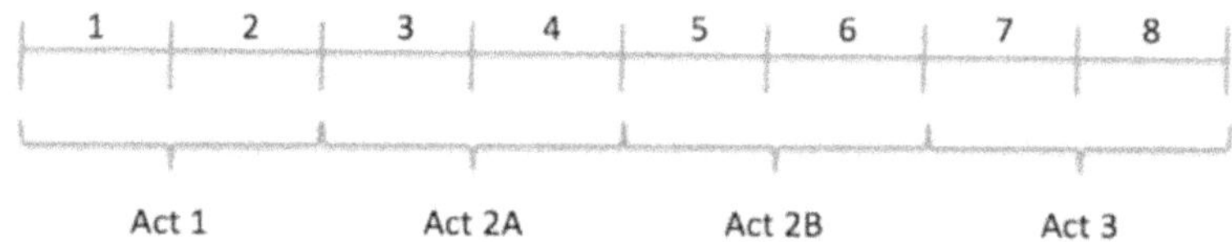

I recently wrote a coming of age story titled, *The Tree Jumper*. It's about Jeremy, who is a geeky X-game enthusiast that falls in love with the head football cheerleader, Brianna. He struggles to understand the unconditional love his blind grandmother teaches him Brianna deserves, compared to the conditional love she receives from her quarterback and football MVP boyfriend.

Here is how the story unfolds in eight major sequences:

S1: Jeremy uses his X-gaming skills to "soar" anonymously through the trees to save the MVP's life during the football team's team building rafting disaster.

S2: Jeremy becomes infatuated with Brianna and encourages her to enjoy "flying" in her cheerleading maneuvers, rather than being confined to the bottom of the pyramid by her fears.

S3: Jeremy learns that Brianna is dating the MVP and awkwardly tries to learn what it takes to court a girl so he can say and do the right things to win Brianna's love away from her uncaring boyfriend.

S4: Chloe adores Jeremy so much that she agrees to help him win Brianna based on whom he is, not old customs from days gone by.

S5: Jeremy becomes confident enough that he shares his love for Brianna publicly and brings the wrath of the MVP down on himself.

S6: The MVP and key players from his football team go out of their way to stop Jeremy from winning Brianna.

S7: Jeremy realizes that true unconditional love would free Brianna to choose whomever she desires to love and would honor her choice. He walks away so the MVP can continue his relationship with her.

S8: The MVP takes Brianna on a joy ride to help her break her fear of heights in his family Cessna and crashes in the trees hanging precariously over the gorge just out of the fire department's reach. Only Jeremy, the tree jumper, can get to the plane and saves both Brianna and the MVP. Brianna has a blast "soaring" through the trees to safety and realizes that Jeremy's love for her isn't conditional like the MVP's.

Each sequence breaks the story into manageable bites and is structured to fit the new 8-segment format for a movie of the week. It also establishes the proper parameters and durations for the three-act structure that feature films use.

And all this, because someone delivered 15 minutes worth of film on a 20-minute reel just shy of a hundred years ago.

Set Pieces Make Films Stand Out

Gaffers, Best Boys and Set Pieces are terms unique to the film industry. Over the decades we learned that a Gaffer is the Chief Lighting Director or the Head Electrician, and a Best Boy is an assistant to either the Chief Electrician or the Key Grip (Head of the Grip department). But "Set Pieces," we thought were pieces of stage scenery.

Set pieces are scenes that are designed to have an obvious imposing effect on the audience and are ideal for trailers. They are also the scenes that stand out and say this film is unique and special. When done correctly, the scenes are easily remembered and create a buzz that drives people to see the movie.

Just about every movie is made up of Shakespeare's three-act structure, which includes a short beginning and ending, and a long middle. Because films tended to die in the long second act, which is about half the length of a typical film, screenwriters split the second act into two segments: 2A and 2B. This was a natural decision as directors constantly wanted to do something special at the film's midpoint.

While the three-act structure is written in four segments, each including two sequences, the responsibility is on the screenwriter to make sure the format doesn't make the story boring. Thus, set pieces entered the picture.

Movies require a minimum of three set pieces to capture the audience. Some use four due to the split second act, while others try to have one set piece in every sequence. Today, there doesn't seem to be any preset requirement due to the ever-changing variety of set pieces, level of creativity, and amount of budget.

A strong set piece lasts the test of time. Many will remember the light saber battle between Darth and Obi-wan Kenobi in *Star Wars*. Another iconic set piece was the scene where Indiana Jones runs away from the giant boulder. I'll never forget the DeLorean racing across the wet mall parking lot and seeing it vanish into a pair of fire trails in *Back to the Future*.

Set pieces distinguish a film and drive the buzz that skyrockets a title to success. Unfortunately, few screenwriters create such scenes, as it takes a significant amount of time to develop and a vast amount of creativity. For these various reasons, spec scriptwriters rarely write iconic set pieces. However, when they do, numerous contracts follow – something every screenwriter should consider.

The Basics of Screenplay Conflict

Every great film is steeped in conflict. Every bad film lacks conflict. The difference is easy to spot, as the only way to move a story forward in film is through conflict. Or more simply put, conflict is to film what sound is to music. Without it, there is no story worth watching.

When a film uses conflict to grab our thoughts and emotions, we lose track of time during the story's journey. When conflict is not present, it doesn't take long to realize we're sitting in a theater and waiting for the movie to revive itself.

Writer Robert McKee once said, "Story is metaphor for life, and to be alive is to be in seemingly perpetual conflict." For a film to demonstrate an honest moment between characters, it must reflect that basic element of being alive. Conflict must be present to some extent in order for the characters to banter about their topic, or dive more deeply into the unspoken or sub-textual topics presented.

There are three main levels of conflict within a character's life: Inner, personal, and extra-personal.

Inner Conflict

This conflict is built within the character's consciousness. The battle takes place in the mind or the spiritual realm. It can be motivated by love or pain, and it must drive visible actions for the viewing audience to understand the character's plight.

Intra-Conflict

This conflict is more dramatic and resides within the relationships of each character and how he or she plays off of the protagonist. It is born out of the inner circle of the protagonist's relationships. The focus rests on the more outward expressions of the relationships and how they unfold within the story.

Inter-Conflict

This conflict is made up of everything that is outside of the character's soul and relationships. It encompasses the entire world surrounding the character, including circumstances and outward interference.

Based on the three above forms of conflict, every scene can explore one or more of the categories. Each conflict can include shifts in power, which might play out as a change in attitude or an exchange of which character is driving the conversation. In the case of inner conflict, the power exchange may show up in the character's actions not matching up with his words – saying one thing, while doing another.

It's my belief that the stronger the conflict, the more interested the viewer is in finding out the ramifications of the exchange. This drive to understand how it will resolve builds the desire within the audience to watch the next scene in hopes of finding the answer. Therefore, the greater the conflict, the greater the need for resolve, causing the viewer to be engaged in the story and lose track of time.

Stories that do not have good conflict are dead and tend to bore the audience during the Second Act. Those that have watched such films and voiced their approval for the story are typically individuals that actually tolerated an inadequate story in the name of a cause or something higher than themselves. They typically speak to the concept or the idea the film held, rather than the quality of the production or performance.

Conflict is a must for every great story. Without it, the stories lack honesty and integrity. For instance, a story of redemption will not work if the protagonist is a good person that gets better. It is only an honest portrayal of redemption if the protagonist starts out marred by his bad choices, as demonstrated on screen.

Unfortunately, many family or Christian moviegoers have adverse reactions to films with flawed protagonists, forcing some filmmakers to tell weaker stories. The opposite is also true. The secular or general moviegoer can't stand films that are about good people that get better because it is not natural or realistic in life. They see it as a false appearance of life, and every message within those films is immediately discounted for its dishonest portrayal.

The only course a filmmaker has to get a healthy message to a general audience is to make a secular film with an honest moral message at the heart of it. However, it might be difficult to find investors for such a story, as the film would feel foreign to Christian investors and questionable to secular investors. However, it would make for the best story for all audiences.

Five Clear Visual Story Conflicts

Independent filmmakers might suggest problems with their movie stem from a low budget and low production values, but the most notable issue comes from the film's lack of conflict. Conflict is the core element of drama. Without it, the film is merely a narrative with no power, traction or energy.

Conflict occurs when two characters (the protagonist and the antagonist) have mutually exclusive, contrasting objectives simultaneously. Only one character can win and the conflict comes when each character does what it takes to make sure they succeed at accomplishing their objective.

There are five types of conflict that can be played visually:

Internal Conflict

Any form of story that touches on the character's self-esteem creates an inner conflict. This can be played out as insecurity, him being unsure of himself, or second-guessing his actions. Many times it is revealed through a conversation with a confidant.

Relational Conflict

The most used form of conflict is reflected in the struggles of the protagonist and antagonist attempting to achieve his goals, which typically rises from their relationship as they attack their mutually exclusive objectives. The protagonist and the antagonist can both be good people, but their separate objectives contrast each other and therefore only one can win.

Societal Conflict

This is like the David versus Goliath type story with a character battling against the government, a group, or a system.

Natural Conflict

Characters are typically thrust into this type of conflict through natural disasters and they find themselves battling the elements. These types of man against "nature" films require large physical or CGI effects. The greatest concern with this type of conflict is that most stories need a secondary relationship-based conflict to cause the audience to care about the outcome.

Supernatural Conflict

This conflict is also known as man against god. It is all about the protagonist battling against an invisible being like the devil or some other supernatural force. To make this type of conflict more visual, stories tend to show the protagonist projecting his problems onto another character.

For these types of conflicts to work, the protagonist must have an opposing character or force that is an equal opponent or adversary. The more clearly this relationship between the protagonist and antagonist is displayed, the stronger the conflict will be – driving the drama to its highest level.

The conflict must also be visual and cannot be avoided. For Hitchcock's knife scene in Psycho to work, the audience had to see the knife coming down into the shower curtain. However, they didn't need to see it pierce the woman, but they did need to see the blood going down the drain.

In an independent film I watched, a man lost his loving wife to a car accident that the audience didn't see. The scene was not emotionally charged or dramatic in any sense of the matter. This was due to the scene not being visual.

Conflict can't be avoided in a drama, but it can be off screen if the audience can see the reaction to the situation through the eyes of another character. The independent film I've referenced could have been very dramatic had the husband heard screeching tires, turned to look, and then recoiled in shock as the audience heard the thud of a body hitting the car.

The visual tells us how dramatic the moment is and how it should impact our emotions. If the visual is not present in some form, there is no drama. This is of course why there are many problems translating a good book to the screen. It also explains why many faith-based films fall flat, when the filmmaker tries to avoid the visible conflict in order to keep the film "clean" for all ages.

Raising the Question

The old rooftop in Greek town with the Chicago skyline for a backdrop, served as a great location for my film project. The shoot was interrupted several times as the "Bat-helicopter" flew overhead shooting background plates for *The Dark Knight*. Chicago had once again become the home of Gotham City and since the production team had precedence over the area, I thought it was best to join them.

Being in the movie made for some very long days, but more importantly I was thankful for the opportunity to learn from director Christopher Nolan and cinematographer Wally Pfister. While Wally and I shared a good laugh about Chicago's ever changing lighting conditions, I learned that Nolan's drive was to keep the story interesting by raising questions within the minds of the viewer.

Most filmmakers are aware that raising a universal question during Act 1 is critical to keeping the audience's attention. By placing a central question during the set-up that resolves during the climax, the storyteller is able to keep the interest of the audience for the duration of the film. The viewer holds tight to his seat until he is able to answer the question residing in the forefront of his mind.

Nolan stepped up the mystery by raising numerous questions to drive the audience from scene to scene. Questions were crafted out of the action plot conflict, interaction between characters, and artistic cinematography. The opening sequence was loaded with various questions and caused the audience to ask who of the clowns was gong to survive, and if one of the survivors would be the Joker.

As the movie opened, the viewer questioned what he should be looking at, as the camera glided over the towers. Nolan answered the question with a window shattering.

```
DAYLIGHT.  Moving over the towers of downtown
Gotham… Closing in on an office building… On a
large window… Which SHATTERS to reveal –
```

The next shot was tight on a smoking gun. The viewer questioned if the Joker held the gun. Nolan then revealed that two men were in the room wearing clown masks.

```
INT. OFFICE, HIGH RISE – DAY

A man in a CLOWN MASK holding a SMOKING
SILENCED PISTOL ejects a shell casing. This is
DOPEY. He turns to a second man, HAPPY, also in
a clown mask, who steps forward with a CABLE
LAUNCHER, aims at a lower roof across the
street and FIRES a cable across.
```

The action shifted the viewer's question to learn what the clowns were up to and where they were going. After a cool shot of the two clowns sliding across the cable to the lower roof, Nolan cut to a street scene and raised another question – Is this the Joker?

```
EXT. DOWNTOWN GOTHAM – DAY

A MAN on the corner, back to us, holding a
CLOWN MASK.
```

In the remainder of the five and a half minute opener, several more questions were raised. The series of rapid questions heightened the curiosity of the viewer and drove the pulse of the opening. It also raised the universal question about how crazy the Joker was or to what extreme he would go. Once the viewer was questioning the Joker's sanity, Nolan launched the final sequence.

INT. LOBBY, BANK – DAY

BOZO slides a GRENADE into the man's mouth. A PURPLE THREAD is knotted around the pin.

BOZO
I believe that what doesn't kill you…

BOZO pulls off his MASK. THE JOKER.

THE JOKER
…simply makes you stranger.

The Bank Manager's eyes go wide. The Joker rises, strolls toward the bus, the purple thread attached to the grenade pin UNRAVELING FROM THE PURPLE LINING of his jacket as he walks. The Joker climbs into the bus, SHUTS the rear door, TRAPPING THE PURPLE THREAD…

As the bus pulls out, the purple thread PULLS THE PIN. The grenade doesn't explode, but SPEWS RED SMOKE.

As the sequence concluded, Nolan revealed that the Joker was sane enough to mastermind an incredibly timed out and intricate plan, including the camouflaged escape with the bus slipping into a line of buses as squad cars zoomed toward the bank.

At the end of the sequence, the viewer knew that the Joker was crazy and sane enough to mastermind anything. The final question left in the viewer's mind – What was the Joker going to do next and would Batman be able to stop him?

The film watcher was hooked and needed to see the remainder of the film to find the answer.

Few independent films define a universal question to entice the viewer to stick around for the answer. Even fewer films use mini questions to increase the viewer's desire to watch the next scene. One of the differences between a good movie and a great movie is raising the curiosity of the audience to the point where they feel compelled to watch the next scene.

When a strong question is raised, viewers find it difficult to step away from the film. Even at home, few will hit the pause button until they get their questions answered.

A simple exercise to test the raising of questions in a film is to pause the movie at the end of every scene and ask oneself what the question is that resides in the viewer's mind. If it isn't obvious, there is a gap in the story that will allow the viewer's mind to drift into boredom.

Drive the Plot with Jeopardy

For years, screenwriters searched for new ways to put the protagonist or hero into jeopardy to drive the plot forward. It's so common that many writers lost track of the one key element that makes it effective – making sure the audience cares about the hero first.

For the audience to care about the hero, there has to be a scene that bonds the audience to the main character. This bonding scene can use a shared crisis or humorous moment to help the audience care about the character to the point of being emotionally invested in his outcome — an overflow of a well-developed character.

Back to the Future, a Michael J. Fox vehicle, endeared the audience to the main character enough to drive a trilogy. In fact, it was the first sci-fi film I remember seeing that made the audience care deeply about the hero and raised the stakes to the point where the audience was emotionally invested in the story.

Once this bond is set in place, the screenwriter can use the same seven ways to raise the stakes in their movie. Each of these I discovered while studying *Back to the Future*: Instinct to Survive, Need for Safety/Security, Desire to Love and Belong, Self-Esteem Lift, Desire to Quench Insatiable Curiosity, Need for Balance in Life, and Expression of Self-Realization.

Instinct To Survive

Life against death is the baseline for the survival scenario. While most films don't push the extreme, many find a way to put the hero in a form of jeopardy that would dramatically change their lives to a point where they might not survive. In *Back to the Future*, the mere sending of Marty back in time was sufficient. He found himself not relating to the things we take for granted.

When Marty found himself in the diner needing to order a drink, he asked for a Tab. The server pointed out that he couldn't have a tab (or bill) until he ordered something. Marty then asked for a Pepsi Free, but the server balked, saying if he was going to order something, he'd have to pay for it. Reluctant to ask for anything else specific, Marty asked for "something without sugar" and was promptly served a cup of coffee.

It didn't take long for Marty to realize that he needed to be careful about his comments and what he shared with others in order to survive his stay in 1955. Most of his mistakes were common practices of the audience in 1985, helping them to bond with him all the more. They understood how easy it would be to make the same errors as Marty.

However, the screenwriter put in place a stronger survival mechanism to drive the action plot. A photo of Marty's family slowly erased because his time travel interfered with history, causing his mom and dad to never meet or kiss for the first time, thus erasing his and his siblings' existence. Marty then scrambled to get his future mom and dad to meet and kiss the night of the dance or history would have been changed, threatening his own existence – a powerful point of jeopardy, driving the film's progress.

Desire to Love and Belong

Another universal point of jeopardy is associated with our longing to be loved and accepted. Humans will go to great lengths to secure love for another and will fight anything that tears away the sense of belonging to something important or someone special. This point can be shown in the form of community, team spirit, romantic interests or traditional family.

The key is in developing the desire to love and belong is to paint a picture for which others can hope or have experienced at some point in their life. Marty found this sense of family while bringing together his mom and dad, working with Doc Brown on time travel, and interacting with Jennifer, his love interest.

Self-Esteem Lift

Most individuals want to be admired. They want to be recognized and respected among their peers. There is a natural, innate desire to be recognized for our life skills, talents and contributions. Humans want to be somebody.

In *Back to the Future,* a healthy form of self-respect or self-esteem would have allowed George to win Lorraine's love, regardless of Biff's behavior. That particular natural drive is significantly different than the need to belong or be loved. It is the inertia that causes one to take action for something in which he believes or desires to possess. Putting the very essence of this gut-felt understanding into the hands of the person with whom the relationship is jeopardized drives the hero into action, to protect himself or the one he loves.

In *Back to the Future,* Marty had to work diligently with George to raise his self-esteem to get George to ask Lorraine to the dance. Marty did that to save his own destiny from being erased from existence. He had no choice but to work with George, even though at the time he seemed beyond help.

Desire to Quench Insatiable Curiosity

No matter how often we try to snuff or coax it, some level of curiosity always drives human behavior. Most of us have an unending need to know and understand who we are and how we fit together with others. Deep within us is a natural instinct to determine how things work and to comprehend how they piece together in our lives. We need to make sure all the pieces of our lives fit harmoniously together to form who we are.

Doc Brown was enticed watching himself on television. It drove a secondary plotline that allowed him to save his own life in 1985 after reading a 1955 letter written by Marty. Doc's curiosity drove him to risk messing up the timeline continuum and alter history. This jeopardy brought a surprise finish to the film and set up several comedic situations.

Need for Balance in Life

Balance is found in people that are secure, confident, and experience love. They hold a sense of balance in their lives and are connected to someone greater than themselves such as a mentor, a wise counselor or God. When this line of connection is broken, the main character feels a dramatic sense of foolish unbalance in his life, creating the right climate to shift the plotline at a moment's notice.

In Act 1 of *Back to the Future,* Marty is a kid misplaced in the wrong home. This cool kid is living among a negative family that seems to be from another planet. The family is out of balance or dysfunctional at best. It sets up many plot points for exploration, as Marty struggles to find harmony within his life. By the end of the film and after a few history-changing events, Marty finds himself in a home with a cool, affirming and positive family.

Expression of Self-Realization

Everyone wants to know ourselves and be who we are. This inner spirit plays out through self-expression and the actualization of our talents and abilities. We find our lives filled with moments when we can hone our skills to match who we see ourselves to be. A comedian has to be funny and entertaining. A doctor has to be logical and methodical. A musician or actor needs to excel at his craft and to please his audience.

In Act 1, we learn that deep within Marty's soul is a musician waiting to be revealed. When this form of self-expression is put in jeopardy, the story takes some interesting turns. Marty finds himself delaying his return to 1985 so he can play one more song in 1955. He had to do it because of who he was. The scene escalated the risk factor of him returning home and drove the film to its climax.

Raise the Stakes

Any of the above areas raises the stakes of the show, but will grip the audience only if they can relate or bond with the character in those moments. Hooking the audience with a more universal stake gives a greater opportunity for driving the plot forward. This can also be accomplished by keeping the character's goal just beyond his reach, causing the audience to strain on his behalf in hopes of subconsciously helping him achieve it.

The more the audience experiences the main character's goal, the more they will connect with him and the easier it will be to drive the plot forward with interesting twists. Playing with the related emotions of the character then allows the writer to play with the audience's emotions as well. Both will find themselves on the same journey. Pulling on these emotional strings will then heighten the jeopardy or raise the stakes for the audience, making the pay-off at the end of the climax of greater value.

Writing a Striking First Image

No matter what camp of writers you follow or attempt to emulate, all know that the opening scene in a feature film must be attention-getting and set the tone for the audience. If it can also introduce the main character, you're one step ahead, but the second scene is sufficient for an introduction.

Big box office screenwriters prefer to leave the main character's introduction for a subsequent scene and focus on what some call the First Strike. Some great examples include J. J. Abram's *Star Trek* reboot, which opens with an attack from a future century Nero that changes the course of history for Kirk and Spock. Typically in the James Bond franchise, the films open with a special 007 mission with cool effects and explosions that aren't necessarily related to the story.

In *The Girl with the Dragon Tattoo,* the opening is of a man that receives a dried flower. The act causes him such great turmoil, he must do something different to bring an end to his pain. This scene doesn't qualify as a First Strike, but rather an emotionally-charged scene, although some might argue that his misunderstanding of who is sending the dried flowers could be construed as a First Strike. The challenge for the screenwriter was to make the first scene into a clear setup for an investigative thriller.

The screenwriter's goal is to make sure he raises a question in the first scene that gives the audience a desire to find the answer as they watch the movie. This technique would be dressed in accordance with the story's theme or genre. The audience expects to be taken to a place they've never been before, or experience something they haven't seen.

If the main character is introduced in the scene, the audience expects to learn something special about the hero or what his typical day looks like. They desire to experience something with him that is either humorous, touching or formulated as a crisis – creating a shared emotion.

These techniques are designed to hook the audience into watching the entire movie and without it; the audience won't suspend disbelief and enter the screenwriter's world. It's therefore important that the screenwriter touches on all the senses by addressing the following elements:

1. Location

2. Time

3. Mood

4. Tone

5. Style

6. Intent

7. Atmosphere

These important elements, coupled with raising the key universal question that drives the audience to seek the answer, will entertain and hook the audience long enough for the screenwriter to get through the needed backstory. It will also give the audience the confidence that they are watching a film worth their time.

Creating A Scene with Nuances and Subtext

When developing a story, the writer needs to decide what a given scene is about. Let's say it's about Mick (**M**ost **I**mportant **C**haracter **K**now) and Sue (**S**ubtle **U**ndermining **E**vildoer), meeting in a laundromat. Since Sue is subtle in her approach, she needs to try and win Mick's attention one small step at a time.

Using the above thoughts, the first draft might come across like this:

```
INT. LAUNDRY MAT – NIGHT

Standing at a folding table, Mick sets down his
excess washer tokens and counts the dryer
tokens.  He is short, again.

Drawing close to Mick, Sue holds out a few
dryer tokens.

                      SUE
           I'm short washer tokens.
           Wanna trade?

Mick pushes washer tokens across the table
toward Sue with his ring finger.

                      SUE (CONT'D)
           Married?

He gives her a weak smile.

Sue gently turns his wrist over and carefully
places the dryer tokens in his hand.  She
gently pulls back, her fingertips grazing his
ring.

                      SUE (CONT'D)
           Looks a little dull.
```

MICK
I'm committed.

SUE
(smiles)
For now.

Sue walks away with gently swinging hips.
The corner of Mick's smile turns up.

The sample subtext scene accomplishes our goal of having Sue subtly approach Mick one step at a time. If she were to come out and say let's have some fun tonight, he wouldn't have any interest. But, the subtle approach allowed Sue to test Mick's perception of his marriage and how soon he might consider trading in for another model.

The scene is also loaded with symbolism and visuals. Since the best scenes are those that live up to the saying, "show, don't tell," the scene plays out well cinematically and subtly. This technique also speaks well to subtext.

The below includes the real unspoken story in brackets:

INT. LAUNDRY MAT – NIGHT

Standing at a folding table, Mick sets down his excess washer tokens and counts the dryer tokens. He is short, again.
[Mick can't seem to win.]

Drawing close to Mick, Sue holds out a few dryer tokens.
[Sue is interested in Mick and will make him a winner.]

SUE
I'm short, washer tokens.
Wanna trade?
[Sue wants Mick, but the choice is his.]

Mick pushes washer tokens across the table toward Sue with his ring finger.
[Mick wants Sue, but he is married.]

SUE (CONT'D)
Married?
[Sue confirms her understanding.]

He gives her a weak smile.
[Mick wishes it were not so.]

Sue gently turns his wrist over and carefully places the dryer tokens in his hand.
[Sue wants to make Mick a winner anyway.]

She gently pulls back, her fingertips grazing his ring.
[Sue wants Mick to know his wife doesn't make him a winner.]

SUE (CONT'D)
Looks a little dull.
[Sue checks to see if Mick knows he can't win with his wife.]

MICK
I'm committed.
[Mick clarifies that it's not about winning, he can't trade for another model.]

SUE
(smiles)
For now.
[Sue let's Mick know she will make him a winner anyway.]

Sue walks away with gently swinging hips.
[Sue lets Mick know his future benefits for trading.]

The corner of Mick's smile turns up.
[Mick is fine with being a winner.]

Sometimes it's good to write the subtext to make sure the scene plays the way it was designed. This can help the writer quickly tweak the story or the subtext that each phrase generates.

In the above scene, we see Mick struggling with his dull life. This is followed by an emotional shift, which leaves Mick filled with the possibilities of being lifted out of his quagmire. The audience now knows that Mick isn't where he wants to be and is tempted by the possibility of change. We also know that his need for change is greater than the pain of change.

With one simple scene built with nuances and subtext, the audience has learned more about Mick than their childhood neighbors. They have also picked up on the question that was embedded into the scene: Will Mick give in to Sue's promises for a better life or stay true to his marriage?

By raising a question at the end of the scene, the audience is compelled to watch more of the movie until he or she gets the answer. They need to know if he is a moral man or one who will do anything to get ahead. This also causes the audience to become invested in Mick and may even feel compelled to cheer Mick on by the third act.

The power of nuances salted into a scene with subtext driving the story, makes for an interesting and entertaining scene. And, by adding in conflict, which in this case is Sue's goal for a man who is already married, can up the stakes and increase the audiences' interest in the rest of the film.

Here is the same scene written by a beginning screenwriter, which lacks nuances and subtext:

INT. LAUNDRY MAT – NIGHT

Mick stands dejected, counting and recounting his tokens. He is short a few dryer tokens.

Sue walks up to him with extra dryer tokens.

SUE
You can have my extra dryer tokens.

MICK
Thanks.

SUE
I'm short washer tokens. Do you have any extras I could have?

Mick hands her his extra tokens.

SUE (CONT'D)
That's really sweet of you. Thanks.

Mick smiles.

SUE (CONT'D)
(smiles)
Are you interested in some coffee, while our clothes tumble?

MICK
No thanks. I'm married.

SUE
Let me know if you ever change your mind. I do my wash here every week.

Sue walks away, then turns back to see if he's looking.

The corner of Mick's smile turns up.

In this version, the same key elements are in place, but the scene carries a very different tone. While the audience will still get the point, it won't drive their desire to see the rest of the film. Nor will it cause the audience to become invested in Mick.

The scene plays flat because it is. The only fix is to heighten the emotions and raise the question. However, those things can only be done successfully using nuances and subtext.

How to Determine Scene Length

Comparing the *Indian Jones: The Last Crusade* screenplay to *Avatar,* it is obvious the length of scenes has greatly shortened over time. Audience attention spans being greatly reduced over the past two decades might have something to do with it, but even with the cutting edge action in *Indiana Jones,* many of the scenes would be considered too long for today's audiences.

During the screenplay workshops I've conducted worldwide, one question arises in the middle of every session, "How long should I make the scene?" No one likes my answer, "As long as it needs to be in order to tell your story in the best way possible, but not long enough to bore your audience." I've never been thanked for that advice, no matter how much the questioners accept the truth of it.

Some guidelines to help writers calculate the answer for themselves are:

Place One Key Storyline Point Per Scene

Every writer I've met has struggled with this concept because most think that in order to make a great film every scene needs to be complex and filled with information. However, the simpler the scene, the easier it is for the audience to follow complex ideas. It is best to simply break up a three-point scene into three scenes.

Focus On Main Character's Goal

Most long scenes grow longer when the writer loses track of the actor's goal and starts developing a supporting character to the same level as the main character. Writers sometimes forget that the only reason a supporting character is in a film is to reveal something about the main character. By focusing on the main character's goal, the story shifts attention to important things, clarifying the message.

Before and After Scenes Matter

Every story has a pace and rhythm that shows up in the length of the film's scenes. If a scene falls into a faster section of the story, the scene will be just as short as the ones surrounding it. If it is in the middle of more relaxed paced scenes, it will conform to a similar length. The exception is when a scene is inserted to change the film's pace.

If during a high action sequence the writer feels a need to let the audience breathe, he inserts a longer scene to accomplish the task, something such as the lull before a storm. The opposite can also be effective when a short scene is slipped in between scenes representing a more status quo type of pace. A change of pace will provide an emotional jolt to regain the audience's attention.

Everything Is Said That Needs To Be Said

Expanding a scene just because the writer likes it is the kiss of death, especially in Act 2, when stories have a tendency to die on their own. Once all the right information is in the scene, it will be the right length, unless the writer added in all kinds of unnecessary and irrelevant information.

Subtext Clarity is Crucial

The more obvious the scene, the shorter it can be. However, the more subtext used, the more interesting the scene, the longer it should be to provide time for needed interchange. During the age of "the shorter the scene the better," writers sometimes forget that a scene twice as long with great subtext passes quicker than a short scene written on the nose.

Motion pictures are a collaboration of the arts and sciences. This overarching fact gives rise to the screenwriter who must put his heart on the page, while scientifically structuring it in a way the audience can receive and be moved by the message. The same holds true for the length of scenes.

The writer must find the exact length that allows him to share his passionate message, while keeping the audience entertained. That perfect balance, achieved by less than ten percent of the screenplays I read annually, makes the difference between a great film worth watching numerous times and a mundane one.

Six Steps to Avoid Shelving A Script

With the year in full swing, screenwriters are typing at a maddening pace to create their greatest story to date. Their compulsion and passion will drive them to create yet another story that will sit on the shelf, an unread masterpiece that doesn't fit any need of the 1,000 cable networks desperate for good stories.

I heard that in 2011 over 10,000 scripts were considered in Hollywood for the silver screen, but less than 400 were given a green light to be made into motion pictures. Add to that the numerous scripts written for cable and syndicated stations that didn't get produced, and you begin to wonder why screenwriters choose to write complete scripts to shop around rather than pitching a quality treatment.

Disney is known for approving films based on a three-page treatment, an handful of storyboards, and an art board or two that captures the essence of the film's style. The sheer passion of the writer's pitch coupled with the aforementioned materials is sufficient to solidify the idea and move the discussion into a development deal.

Even with the system seeking ideas, concepts and treatments, screenwriters continue to crank out 120 pages of script that will likely never be read. Instead, the writer should align with the industry and give consideration to the six steps below that will often lead to a successful script:

Step One

Write a three-page treatment that captures the thrill of the story. Write it like an around the campfire cliffhanger grabbing the attention of fellow campers.

Step Two

Write the beginning of the story to captivate the audience with the energy catapulting them into the middle of the story. This requires a high concept idea introduced with a "wow" factor opening.

Step Three

Create a main character that every name actor in the business wants to play and put him on a journey that brings about positive change in his life.

Step Four

Practice by pitching the story to friends. Make sure it grabs and keeps their attention. Bring them to the edge of their seats as you move your story to its climax. Then give them a pleasant resolve that allows them to breathe again.

Step Five

Rewrite your treatment based on the elements that worked and quickly toss the segments that went flat. If you can't tell the story with excitement, it won't read well for studio executives.

Step Six

Pitch the story to the right network. If your story is about men playing poker, it wouldn't be wise to pitch it to the Lifetime network, as they look for heartfelt stories with strong female leads. Nor would an intense dramatic thriller be appropriate for Nickelodeon.

While treatments are great for moving your discussion toward development, you will eventually need to write the screenplay. Some professionals keep at least one screenplay in the works on a quarterly basis and have at least one treatment being tweaked weekly.

Every writer must find his or her own pattern and take time to manage the business side of selling the script. Few agents today find work for their clients, forcing writers to own the outcome of their own businesses.

Keeping Act 2 Alive

It's been said all too often that if a film is going to die, it will be in Act 2. Of course, the reason it's stated so often is because it's true. There are several reasons for this prophetic Act 2 nightmare:

- Writers that lose focus stray from the spine of the story or distort the through line during the longest act.
- Writers sometimes stick in favorite scenes that don't fit the story.
- They get into creating dialog instead of action.
- Then also lose track of the stories pace and slow down the story, or speed it up so fast that the audience can't learn about the characters.

The only way to avoid these issues is to write, keeping with the story's momentum. Every scene participates in the momentum of the story by setting up the main character's goal, which leads to his action, which forces a reaction or a complication and drives the audience the next scene.

This cause and effect, or action and reaction pattern, moves the story to the next scene in an interesting way that draws the audience deeper into the story. These complications can be in the form of:

- Barriers that must be overcome or skirted
- Delayed pay-offs of the action points
- Reversals that change the direction of the story

The reversal is typically used at one of the turning points or at the midpoint in film.

There are several test questions you can ask yourself as you evaluate each scene for its potential addition or subtraction to the story's momentum.

1. Does the story gain momentum through action or does dialog force it to advance?
2. What types of complications are in the story and where are they located?
3. Are the complications organic to earlier dramatic elements in the story?
4. Are scene sequences used to set up the complications?
5. Is the scene aligned with the through line?

The key is that all actions in a story must be connected to the through line and to the action that precedes it and follows it. It would be prudent for writers to also remember that dialogue can take away from momentum and should therefore be used sparingly.

Rewriting the Rewrite

Rewriting the short film *Family Law* consumed my time a few years back, but it was worth the effort once the film festival season began. The film took home numerous awards including: Best Screenplay and Best Actress. Family Law provides good examples for the rewriting process.

The premise of the film is that law firm partner Carol Peters fights to keep legal sharks away from a teenage boy that wants emancipation from his oppressive home life. Cornered by the boy's choice, Carol risks disbarment unless she can find the deal-changing answer in a gentle whisper.

During the rewriting process, I had numerous conversations with a copy editor and the film's star, Francine Locke. Both were experts in their fields, but neither fully comprehended the rewriting process. In fact, while Francine loved the overall story, she felt the dialogue was too "in her face and wordy," as it was in the draft she reviewed.

I explained the process to her and pointed out how in the first draft I tend to write the dialogue "on the nose" to make sure I understand what information needs to be presented to the audience. It's not until a later draft, when I deal with subtext, that I rewrite the dialogue. The explanation caused me to realize that many beginners in the industry may not have handles on the rewriting process, so I decided to share a five thoughts that will help the rewriting process:

1. Rewrite for Excellence

I haven't met a writer who didn't love their first draft. This is a byproduct of a writer's attempt at reducing their great story ideas to writing. However, as a script doctor, I've had to inform many writers that their job wasn't done after the first few drafts. It takes several attempts to get the writer to realize that he only placed the foundation of the story on the page and not the fully envisioned movie.

Through self-examination of my emotions and a second objective look at my story, I found that my first draft scripts aren't close to what they're meant to be. The reality is that while my story concept starts to surface in the first draft, the rest of the story needs to be fleshed out through additional rewrites.

A few years back, I was invited to an awards ceremony at the Beverly Hills Hotel, which gave me an opportunity to chat with two Oscar-winning writers of the movie *Cars*. They shared how it took them three years to rewrite the story with some scenes having as many as 22 rewrites, winning them an Oscar and a sequel.

2. Throw Away the First Draft

After my final rewrite of *Family Law,* I realized there were no sentences from my first draft that survived and there were only a few sentences from my second draft remained unchanged. I could have easily thrown out the first draft and started over with a better chance of achieving my story goals.

Unfortunately, most writers fight to keep as much of their original writing in tact. This lowers the quality of their story and blinds them from an opportunity of telling the story from a better perspective or from another character's point of view. My first draft of *Family Law* was about the teenage boy, but I found a stronger story by shifting the perspective to the female lawyer.

Jack B. Sowards, known for his television Emmy winning scripts, wrote *Star Trek: The Wrath of Khan*. Until the J.J. Abrams Star Trek reboot, Jack's story about Khan was considered by fans as the best Star Trek story out of the dozen features released. Jack is a man dedicated to quality and as a matter of practice; he literally gets up out of his chair, walks over to the wastebasket and drops his first draft in.

3. Rewrite the Good to make it Great

The main reason actress Francine Locke decided to produce *Family Law* was a desire to find a creative vehicle that could feature her talents at festivals. This type of pressure might typically cause a writer to make only slight adjustments to a script, missing an opportunity of making it great. I've personally learned that greatness can happen only when the writer is willing to scrap what is good to make room for what is great.

Just about everyone wanted me to change the climax in *Family Law* to make it bigger, but they missed the important fact that it needed to be realistic, plausible and lead to the resolve. While I accepted some rewrite recommendations, I chose to hold to my third draft version of the climax. The result during sneak previews, I watched every person tear up during the climax, proving that a writer should rewrite only what he or she agrees would improve the story, not just change the whole thing.

4. Be Clear, Not Obvious

Every rewrite should help clarify the story and main character. It's important to keep the audience in the emotional flow of the story and not bog them down with huge backstory or "in your face" dialog. The writer's focus should be on bringing out the characters and plot, rather than muddying the waters with attempts at iconic phrases like "I'll be back." French writer Gustave Flaubert suggested that the "artist should be felt everywhere and seen nowhere."

In *Family Law,* I found myself writing what I perceived as a perfect climax and resolution, but some people were concerned that the audience might not catch the visual nuances that turn a story into a grand slam. Francine even asked if I should write a more obvious ending. However, with me being a person that always understands a film well before the writer hits me over the head so I "get" his story, I decided to trust that my audience would be more visually intelligent than not. I kept my ending.

5. Take Time for another Rewrite

Going into a film project with a goal of seven plus rewrites helps me to depersonalize the story and see it objectively. While I'm not suggesting that my passion drops during the process, I am being realistic about the numerous drafts that lead to a successful story. Many screenwriting consultants have been quoted saying, "Screenwriting is not about writing, but rewriting."

The script supervisor from *Family Law* asked her screenwriting professor about the number of rewrites it takes to make a good script great. The professor cited a student that did two rewrites, and then sold the script to a production company, which then did two more rewrites before production. While the professor suggested that four rewrites was all that was necessary, the script supervisor couldn't help but wonder what the minimum number of rewrites would be to guarantee a strong and tight story.

Family Law, a six-minute short film, took five rewrites to pull on the heartstrings of the audience and deliver the theme to their hearts. Had it been a feature, I'm sure the rewrites would have been well over a dozen or two.

I learned a long time ago that rewrites are not something to avoid, especially since the WGA makes sure you get paid well for rewrites. Instead, it is a tool to double check the tightness of your characters, plots and subplots, emotional patterns, dialogue, etc. If each rewrite focuses in on just one area of a script like format, continuity, visualization, etc. it would take a minimum of a dozen rewrites to make sure every aspect of a script is excellent.

The script writing process is all about rewriting. The fear of having too many rewrites is held only by beginners, as the professional counts on polishing each aspect of his story through the rewriting process. When you have a powerhouse actor on your film project like Tom Hanks, you plan on lots of extra rewrites to live up to his excellence in performance. Tom Hanks' *Cast Away* saw 250 rewrites over five years before he was ready to film. That abundance of rewriting led to 22 nominations and 11 awards.

Telling A Story that Inspires Faith and Action

Many faith and values films are actually religious films in disguise. They are typically written, directed and produced by a person who has a specific message to get across. He typically desires to use film rather than a pulpit, and isn't well versed in the craft of storytelling. In chats with these types of filmmakers, I attempt to share how they can integrate a message into a great story, rather than attach a story to a message.

The first rule is to make sure the main plot is filled with some form of a protagonist or hero taking some proactive action, which is why it's called the "action plotline." The second rule is that the message can never be a part of the action plotline, but must be a part of the "B" plotline.

The typical argument I get is that the message is very important and therefore needs to be in the action plotline instead of a secondary plotline. However, while a book might be able to succeed in this manner, films typically fail. The reason for this consistent failure is due to messages being good or wholesome, while action plotlines need conflict and consequences to survive and progress.

Rarely will an author risk his key message in a sea of conflict. It's much easier for the hero to learn it during a lull in the action. In this way the hero can find a unique application for it in order to save the day by the end of the film, making the storyline and climax more valuable.

By applying the message through the "B" plotline, the audience gets a glimpse of how to translate the message into their lives. It becomes a demonstration for multiple types of applications based on each viewer's life experience. The message instantly becomes a tool for everyday life.

However, many faith and values filmmakers put the message in the action plotline, which slows down the story and causes the audience to feel preached at. Typical filmgoers are much more open to messages shared with them rather than preached to them.

We all like to hear words of wisdom from a pastor, close friend or mentor that we know wants the best for us. But similar advice from a hero or main character that isn't our friend falls flat unless the words are specifically crafted to connect with us.

This connection is made through a skillful style of writing subtext, requiring the message to be relegated to the "B" plotline. The outcome will not only inspire faith, but will also energize the viewers to consider taking action in their own lives – making the story as well as the message a great experience.

Telling a Cinematic Party-Like Story

I was looking at the cool glass award statue that was delivered for winning "Best Story" at a film festival. Since I'm always interested in how the award winners achieved recognition, I thought I'd share a few thoughts about creating a good story for film.

Soviet Russian film director Sergei Eisenstein was the first to play with film story. He said film story should be told through cuts or the juxtaposition of uninflected images.

If you listen to how a guy tells a story at your next party, you'll hear him share it cinematically. This is partially due to the times we're in, but it's more than that. We tend to jump from one thing to another as we share our thoughts. We piece together a series of individual things we notice and share it in a like fashion.

Maybe he told it like this...

"The sun was really bright. I could barely see through the glare on my windshield. All of a sudden this guy bounced off of the hood of my car. He rolled into the other lane. The woman in the oncoming car slammed on her brakes and stopped within inches of hitting the guy. Then the man got up and walked away. I had no clue who he was or where he came from."

This story was put together by taking different shots or things noticed, and stringing them together so the juxtaposition of the elements told a story. In fact, if the story were broken apart, you could create a shot list:

- Bright sun
- Glare on windshield
- Guy bouncing off hood of car
- Guy rolls into oncoming traffic
- Shocked woman in oncoming car
- Brakes being slammed on
- Car stopping inches from guy
- Guy stands
- Guy walks away

There can certainly be additional shots added to the list depending on the director's desire to show cutaways or reaction shots. He can also be creative in the angles of the shots or in the equipment used to capture the images. However, the most important element is that the story was visual or cinematic.

By creating a cinematic story, we are telling it in a way that anyone can understand, as they would have told the story in the same way at a party. This film language is key to writing good film story, unfortunately, most screenwriters write stories that require narration and dialogue, rather than stories that stand on their own.

The ideal film is the silent one that has been enhanced by some dialogue. This allows the story to be understood regardless of the regional language of those watching it. They can fully understand the story, even if they can't pick up on the nuances sparingly salted in dialogue.

The original screenplay for *Family Law,* my award-winning story, was 40 percent longer than it needed to be, so I cut it dramatically. The goal was to be able to understand the point of the story with the sound off. I believe it was accomplished.

However, since its release, I realized that the story could have been better served with more time analyzing and rewriting the scenes. After all, writing a story in one week and then filming it, probably wouldn't allow the story to be at its best. But in this case, it was strong enough to be recognized at a film festival.

Brand Science Meets Great Storytelling

Product placement has been around since James Dean combed his hair with an ACE Flex pocket comb and company sales quadrupled. Sony, Coke and other big boys immediately jumped on the product placement bandwagon.

Risky Business and *Men in Black II* gave a boost in sales to Ray-Ban sunglasses. *Back to the Future* promoted several Pepsi products. *You've Got Mail* promoted AOL and Starbucks. And, *Cast Away* successfully teamed with Fed Ex and Wilson.

Satires and parodies also jumped into the product placement game with *Wayne's World* and *Josie and the Pussycats*. The latter, having 27 products placed within the film, was a parody of massive proportions.

Michael Bay (*Transformers, Armageddon, Pearl Harbor*) and partner Scott Gardenhour (*Pearl Harbor, Jumper, Coyote Ugly*) came together to create The Institute, a multi-platform media company that integrates creativity with brand marketing. They believe in innovation and finding the right balance between products and story to drive consumer demand.

Filmmakers have always been in need of funds and brand managers have always needed stories to promote their products. Frankly, it makes sense for the two to come together in a way that enhances the story and doesn't detract from it. Bay's Institute is already exploring numerous stories that promote products. They draw the audience into a story that encourages them to accept the product without any real consideration.

Corporations love this new approach as it demonstrates their product in a good light and helps the future buyer remember the product in conjunction with the great feelings the film attributed to it. The key is making sure the right storytellers connect with the right products, to ensure a seamless partnership that everyone accepts without feeling pulled out of the story and into an ad.

This same innovation works in reverse, as Bay made a couple commercials with memorable stories that brought a smile to the viewers face and introduced him or her to a specific product. The Levi product story promotes future dreams and the Audi story promotes a more nostalgic look at love and making the wrong choice.

The more integrated the product is within the story, the greater the ability of the audience to receive the related feelings through future associations – a strong selling point for any product. However, to avoid the story turning into a bad job of product placement, it must be done in an artistic and creative way that moves the story forward.

When successful, everyone accepts the reality of E.T. eating Reese's Pieces. Hershey saw its sales go through the roof with a 65-85 percent increase in sales. To this day, I'm sure Mars is still wondering why that executive turned down Steven Spielberg's request for M&Ms to be in the film.

When story and product match up well, all parties win big. The key is finding the right product that fits the right audience with the right story. Anything less than that makes the sad attempt appear to be a parody without effort, which is a lose / lose scenario for all involved.

Most independent filmmakers can't place products in their stories because they don't take the time to use the science that determines what audience the story is geared toward, let alone what product fits.

Independents love to throw ideas together fast enough to shoot something, rather than planning a story that properly integrates a product with its symbolism and theme. But for the filmmaker that can figure out this new process, they will be in filmmaking for years to come, while others scrape for enough funds to shoot their next picture.

Breaking Screenwriter's Block

I'm often asked what I do to avoid or get out of screenwriter's block. My response is always, "There's no such thing." That response is seldom accepted, as writers like to label what stumps them. At which point I share my differing view and admit that I've never experienced writer's block. Instead, I adjust my perspective to regenerate my creativity.

Here are a few ways I've done it:

Change Perspective

Change your perspective the moment you feel your creative juices slowing down.

I was in a special Bell Labs program where we were asked to come up with 100 different uses for a widget that was put in front of us. Others that participated in the think tank a week earlier came up with only 17 innovative ideas and gave up.

The team I was on immediately came up with 23 ideas and then everyone's ideas, except mine, started to fade. A few people asked why I wasn't stumped. I shared how I thought through everything from my perspective, and then looked at them from the viewpoint of a child. After hitting 56 ideas, I changed my perspective to that of an elderly woman.

Everyone followed suit and we completed the project with 137 innovative ideas. We later learned that the company picked idea number 97, and manufactured the product, making the company millions.

Scribble Down First Thoughts

Before you begin, scribble a bunch of ideas onto paper without much thought.

I worked on an animated project with an expert animator who started his brainstorming process by scribbling doodles onto a plain white piece of paper. He never wanted to start with a blank page, and the scribbles made sure he always started with something.

The first time I scribbled lots of messy lines onto the page, I found three cool characters buried inside of the scribbles. I then went over them with a thicker marker so they would stand out enough for me to transfer the concepts to a clean sheet.

The technique works the same for writers. By reducing first thoughts to writing, the creative person is able to develop a mind map or board ideas that will drive new thoughts and a fresh focus.

Birth New Ideas By Exploring Content

If the content is too short or not entertaining, expand it by asking questions about each existing idea. By asking a "who, what, where, when, why and how" question, the writer is able to see additional possibilities worth exploring. The process can also bring clarity to what elements are most important.

By using a number of techniques to change perspective or the vantage point, the screenwriter is always able to write something – Bringing an end to "screenwriter's block."

Preparing the Elements to Make a Film

Seven Tips Directors Wished Their Writers Knew

A chapter on screenwriting from a director's perspective might seem self-serving, but what I'm sharing quickly differentiates great writers from the really good ones.

These finer points can easily be overlooked by an experienced writer that sees a familiar term and doesn't take time to understand it from the director's perspective. Since the director owns the vision of the film, it's prudent to understand his expectations for a given scene.

The below tips will help writers deliver what the director expects:

1. Improve The Scene, Don't Change It

It's frustrating for a director to read a scene that is just shy of being perfect. Not because the writer missed the mark, but because the director typically gets back significant changes instead of the minor modifications he requests. I've seen stories needing a slight tweak go through such major revisions that it changed a comedy into a drama.

Major changes are typical for writers that love creating story and don't take time to understand what the director was planning to do with a given scene. Before making any changes, writers need to find out what the director likes about the scene and how he perceives it, so they know what not to change. The writer's focus must facilitate the director's vision, not keep her favorite scene intact or create something that could be really cool in a different film.

2. Understand The Point Of The Story

Every writer knows that each scene must move the story forward or be cut from the film. Scenes that are near and dear to the writer's heart, but don't move the audience toward the point of the film, leads to the deterioration of the story. I'm amazed at how many professional writers lose track of the story's point during their creative process and write something that doesn't belong in the film.

It's prudent for the writer to reduce the point of the story to paper and compare it to every scene, making sure it belongs in the film. She might also reconsider arguing with the director about keeping the "unique" scene, as it will weaken the core story and make both of them look bad.

3. Develop Subtext

If I had a dollar for every time a writer is told to write subtext... So why are so few scenes built on subtext? I co-wrote a love story that had a scene with the woman helping the man learn about abductive reasoning while packing for a trip to meet her folks. The original scene was flat and written on the nose, like many first drafts. By having the main character decide about taking or not taking a sweater based on possible weather conditions, we were able to create subtext about how warmly her parents could be expected to receive him..

Creating subtext is an art all unto itself and is welcomed by all directors. One of the easiest ways to create subtext is for the writer to build an honest scenefrom a situation she would normally avoid in life at all costs. By forcing the character through the situation with as much tact as possible, while being honest, the writer will generate a layer of subtext that the director and actors can ignite.

4. Create Clear Story Beats

The term "beats" is hard to explain since there are beats in the three-act structures, beats within a scene, and action beats for actors--not to mention when an actor takes a beat or pauses. Every scene has a beginning, middle and end, which accounts for a minimum of 3 beats. Within each scene are shifts of power between characters that are also called beats.

The key beats that directors look for are the exchanges of power between actors through dialogue or physical movement. These beats set up a rhythm for the scene and bring interest to the viewer. Without the beats, the scene is flat and can lose the audience's attention. Writers that proactively create beats within each scene to capture and recapture the audience's attention are always in high demand.

5. Set The Scene's Rhythm

Story ebbs and flows like an ocean. Each character takes on a life of his own and his interaction drive scenes in new directions, while the writer maintains the point and direction of the overall story. Every conflict or surprise gives rise to another shift or turning point within the story and takes the audience down a path they've never visited before.

There is a natural rhythm that rises from the characters that the screenwriter needs to find and clarify. If forced, the scene becomes stilted and cliché. The writerbrings clarity to these strong and weak patterns to enhance the storytelling process. When that is done properly, the audience feels good about witnessing actions within a scene, drawing them further into the story.

6. Shift Power In Every Scene

Numerous techniques exist that alter the control of power within a given scene. This can be done with blocking, camera position and most importantly, dialogue. Through a handful of expressed words, a writer can take the power owned by one character and quickly pass it to another. In a moment of conflict, the exchange may happen several times, raising the interest of the audience.

The easiest way to shift power from one character to another is by having the one in power ask a question, followed by the other avoiding an answer and talking about another topic. This immediately transitions the power within the scene. Another example is having the person in power make a statement and having the other person immediately accuse the first person.

7. Add More Conflict

Stories are boring without conflict. It doesn't matter if the conflict rises from the internal, nature, or another character. What does matter is that the story must be laced with plenty of it. Too many writers don't want their good character to come across in a nasty way, so they avoid creating moments of conflict. However, great drama is built on conflict and great characters learn how to work through conflict.

The easiest way to overcome a character looking bad for a moment is to focus on the choice and outcome of the conflict. Audiences are intelligent enough to focus on what the writer declares important and avoid going down rabbit trails that don't exist. By establishing a choice or a forced decision, the writer can demonstrate the character of the protagonist as he walks through the difficulties and finds success.

Focusing on these seven tips will bring peace of mind to most directors and save his efforts from having to tactfully hire another writer to improve your story for a strong transition to the screen.

Determine if a Script is Worth Shooting

I've read hundreds of scripts as a festival judge and director over the years and I've found seven steps that help me determine if a script is worth shooting. The seven steps are ideal for assessing if the story is visually compelling with believable characters.

Since I will be writing about the "main character", "protagonist" or "hero" throughout this article, I'll just call him "Mick" (the **M**ost **I**mportant **C**haracter **K**nown) to simplify.

1. The Human Condition

During the first read of the script it's important to recognize if the story points out Mick's natural flaw. Since we're all flawed, the film won't be believable if Mick doesn't have one. Films that have "good" people becoming "better" don't work, as people won't be able to relate to an inauthentic Mick. The script needs a flawed Mick we can embrace.

A great script also reveals what makes Mick do the things he does. These motivations must be presented in a visual manner within the script with lots of verbs, not adjectives. This will give the director a quick handle on how to visualize the exploration of Mick's life.

2. The Action Plotline

The script must be clear about story elements such as who the characters are, the location of the action, what form of growth or change happens to Mick, and so on. After the first read, the following questions should be answered to clarify if the story makes sense:

- What is the story about?
- Can it be explained in two sentences or 30 seconds?
- Was the story easy to follow and understand?
- Are the obvious problems easy to correct?
- What is the theme of the story?
- Can all plotlines be easily listed?
- Can the story beats be easily picked out?
- Does the climax make a profound or emotional impact?

Further analysis may be done on a scene-by-scene basis. The following questions can help determine if a scene might hit the cutting room floor or survive:

- Does the scene raise a question or resolve a previous question?
- In what way does the scene advance the story?
- How many power exchanges are within the scene?
- How often does the emotional status of the scene change?

3. The Motivation

Mick must drive the action plot and require some form of motivation to do so. Reviewing the script elements that drive Mick's behavior to change from his flawed human condition to something greater must be in place for the action plotline to take the audience on a journey.

The script elements must infer what Mick thinks, how he feels, and thereby what actions he takes, which all serve to drive the story forward. To establish Mick's motivation, the script must have some form of objective laced throughout the story. It needs to be clear and concise. The following questions can help determine Mick's motivation:

- What does Mick want to do throughout the story?
- What does Mick want to do in each scene?
- What is Mick doing versus what he is saying?
- How does Mick's choices drive the audience to the next scene?
- What is Mick willing to sacrifice to obtain his objective?

4. The Juxtaposition Of Images

All great films are a series of shots that tell a story. While many think the dialogue is the most important part, it is actually the selection of shots in a series that reveals the essence of the story. My favorite types of films are those that can be watched and understood with the sound turned off. Here is a shot list to make the point:

- A single long stem rose is held behind a man's back.
- A man's hand knocks on a door.
- A woman's hand turns the doorknob.
- The door swings open past long legs and red high heels.
- The rose is pulled out from behind the back.
- A man's hand places the rose into a woman's hand.
- The man's feet fidget.
- The rose flies across the room.
- The rose lands in a wastebasket.

- A woman's hand pushes against a man's chest.
- The man's feet shuffle backwards.
- The door swings closed.

The above shot list was my rendition of Mick trying to make up for a mistake with the woman he loved. The shots suggested that she pushed him back into the doghouse for a bit more time, rejecting his attempt at reconciliation.

The simple positioning of individual shots generates the audience's creativity and allows them to draw on their own emotional backgrounds to understand what the shots meant. If the script doesn't suggest a certain series of visual opportunities in the story, it may be better as a book than a film.

5. The Camera's Perspective

Great scripts hint at camera movement, position and point of view. Bad scripts tell the director what type of shot to use. Determining if the writer is a would-be cinematographer or is excellent at his craft by merely suggesting possibilities will help a discerning director determine the cinematic language of the film.

A helpful script suggests if the camera view is:

- **Objective:** This type of camera positioning gives the audience an outsider's look at the story, as if they were standing at the fourth wall looking on.
- **Subjective:** This placement is typically within the action itself, rather than at a "safe" distance, pulling the audience into the scene. The shaky camera technique is

subjective as it makes the audience feel like they are in the story.

- **POV:** This camera angle is typically set up by a subjective series of shots and then reveals what Mick is seeing.

The emotional tone and pace of the film determines which of the above types of camera shots are best used. Regardless of the suggestion hinted at in the script, the director needs to understand how the shots would drive the central idea or super objective of the story forward. Whatever shots take away from that goal should be changed.

6. The Movement Of Characters

Scenes that suggest movement based on human reactions greatly support the director's vision. Since every director needs to block the actors in relationship to the camera and other characters, any suggested movement within the story would simplify the shoot.

To determine if the story is mostly made up of talking heads or physical action, the following questions can be considered:

- Where was Mick located in the last scene?
- Where will Mick start in the current scene?
- Will the juxtaposition of A and B impact the story?
- In real life, what would Mick's natural movement be in the scene?
- Is Mick increased or diminished in the scene?
- Should Mick be closer to or farther from the camera?
- Would an angle shot increase the emotions of the scene?
- If the scene is intimate, will a steady close-up work?

- If the scene is active, would tight shots increase the emotional intensity or distract the audience from understanding the action?

It's important to understand that the above list is a fraction of the possibilities. It should also be noted that movement could be created by Mick moving or by the director moving the camera.

7. The It

Great films are great because of all the story elements that come together. Scripts that help the director to visualize the location and production design, the cinematography and sound with music and effects, the editing potential and pacing, and anything else highly unique like stunts, special effects, and whatever else will take filmmaking to the next level, all make up the thing we call "it".

The "it" is the synergy that makes the story spectacular, well beyond the sum of the filmic elements that brought the film into being. It is that panache that can't be created, but shows up. Simply put, it is those elements that make the story universal for all audiences, while being specifically unique as if no niche market has ever seen it before.

When a director finds a script that has all seven steps showing up in strength within the story he's considering, he finds his passion for the story growing beyond what he's capable of holding in. He must tell the story. Anything shy of this isn't worth the time or effort.

The Table Read

Many in development neglect the opportunity for a table read of their script. It is a simple step that can feed animatics, if recorded, or just give a reality check to the writer. While the dialogue might not be interpreted the way a director would drive the story, it is still of value in understanding what story elements are clear and what dialogue doesn't work.

The writer, director or producer might call for the table read and contact SAG/AFTRA actors to fill the roles. Sitting everyone in a circle helps each voice to easily be heard. If microphones are being used for recording purposes, it's helpful to give everyone headphones. The use of microphones and headphones helps the actors speak in a more film-like manner and still be heard, regardless of the extreme shout or whisper.

I've found that most actors will do a reading for free if they have a legitimate shot at the role or it gives them an opportunity to work with a director they hope to work with in the future. Relationship building does make for future opportunities. If the person putting the table read together doesn't have the ability to offer the role, then a small stipend is beneficial. If the session is recorded for animatics, it should be treated as a performance with proper pay.

There are two types of table reads. The most common is the straight read-through from top to the bottom of the script. A narrator reads all the actions and headers, and the actors read their roles as it plays out in a linear fashion. This gives everyone a solid understanding of the story, its flow, and many times, its pacing.

The second type of read is conducted on a sequence or scene basis. It is done so immediate fixes can be worked and tested with the actors. During this type of read, actors are asked their opinions for word choice, dialogue flow, and other input to improve the development of the character.

Table reads can have drawbacks, as something can be played flat in a read through that sparkles once put to the right action, camera angle and music. The director uses the table read to find script issues and not assume the read is explicit in how the film will play out.

The reading table is not designed to move toward perfection, but rather catch the unseen mess waiting to happen. It's far cheaper to correct a problem in development than in production, when every hour costs thousands of dollars.

With that perspective in mind, a table read is an excellent tool that would be prudently added to any writer, director or producer's tool belt.

Three Things Directors Do To Help Casting

Casting is all about finding the right actor for the right role at the right time. It is also the first area where newbie directors fail. This might be due to there being a plethora of documentation for the actor's role in casting, but very little for the director. In fact, the few things that can be found are usually for the casting director, not the director.

On bigger pictures, the director works with the casting director, who manages the pre-selection process. They vet principal actors based on schedule, ballpark figures, look, desire to play the role, and their history of playing nice with others. No one wants an actor that is a nightmare waiting to happen on the set.

There are three things directors can do to simplify the casting director's job:

1. Create A Cast Breakdown

The cast breakdown is a one-page document with thumbnail character descriptions. It is not based on the actor's looks, but rather allows the casting director to infer the character's physical appearance and level of attractiveness. Here are a couple examples from my latest list:

ERIC: (26), confident, athletic, intelligent, playboy-esque, chivalric, passionate about truth and justice, explores ideas, fun-loving, yet classy.

KATHY: (25), high intellect, slender, beautiful, nice, gracious, firm, business-like, follows rules.

2. Know Mix and Match Combinations

When working with name talent, timing and money is key to a successful selection. Many times a director is forced to pick an actor that doesn't quite fit the thumbnail, but can draw a larger audience to the box office. In those cases, the director must understand the characters well enough to alter the thumbnails of contrasting or complimentary characters.

3. Develop A Headshot List

Collecting headshots of potential actors for each character will help give the casting director a visual understanding of the director's vision, especially if the headshots clearly compliment the cast breakdown and look the age. I like using Pinterest boards to collect my ideas for casting.

The number of hours required to accomplish the above is dependent on the amount of detail and accuracy the director wants to capture for his casting director. The hardest task is determining the cast breakdown, which newbies tend to overwrite. Here is an example of an overwritten cast breakdown:

ERIC: (26), 6′ tall, wavy brown hair with highlights, muscular athletic build, dimples, blue eyes, sexy smile, confident, womanizer with a look of innocence, chivalric, sharp dresser, intelligent, passionate about truth and justice, explores ideas through experimentation, fun-loving, comical at times, yet classy.

It's important to give the casting director the right vision with the flexibility to search for just the right combination of actors. The better the fit, the more realistic the drama.

Directing a Great Screen Test

In the day and age of uploads, many actors find themselves performing to a camera in their living room and uploading their interpretation of the character. The better the camera, lighting and the actor's understanding of the character, the better chance he or she has of making the cut, or not.

Real screen tests are in person with the director. In fact, I'd say that the process is more about the director than about the actor.

Screen tests are not performances. Screen tests are a part of a process that helps the director determine if the actor has the faith, patience and trust required to build the character according to his vision. The screen test is a tool for the director to assess if the actor has the elements that make the character who and what he is..

Inexperienced directors, who are unsure of the rehearsal and screen test process, often settle for actors that have learned certain skills that present a superficial reality, rather than develop a character that captures the hearts of the audience. When this occurs, the director typically gets whatever they see in the audition in their film, rather than a truth-based, believable character.

Instead, the director should focus on three key audition elements:

The Right Actor For The Right Role

The *Back To The Future* trilogy made box office history because Michael J. Fox was the perfect person to play the role of Marty. His timing was impeccable and his actions were an ideal fit for the character's adventure. However, Eric Stoltz was first hired to play Marty and three weeks into production, Director Robert Zemeckis realized he had hired the wrong actor. He immediately let Stoltz go and hired Fox.

The director's job during the screen test is to make sure he is getting what he thinks he is getting. He needs to work with the auditioning actors and explore the development of the characters using sides. While working with the actor, the director should be asking himself the following questions:

- Do you see the character in the actor?
- If you see a version of the character, is it a version that will work?
- Is the actor interesting to watch?
- Does the actor surprise you with various readings against the original line?
- Do you get drawn into the character or do you see the actor?

If several of the above questions get a positive response from the director, it is a signal that further exploration should take place. However, if most of the above items aren't checked off, the director has one of two choices to make: shoot a film that doesn't match his vision or search for another actor.

A Truthful Performance

Many independent films have good performances, but lack great performances. This is due largely to the fact that middle range actors are readily available and have memorized certain actions, looks or gestures that work on screen, but are superficial. Seldom do independent film budgets allow the director and actor to develop a character that is captivating. Most settle for the memorized gimmicks and quick cuts.

Experienced directors know to look for key abilities in their actors by asking themselves the following questions:

- Does the actor work in the moment?
- Does the actor listen to the director?
- Does the actor listen to the other actors in the scene?
- Does the actor anticipate the line, or allow the circumstances in the moment to prompt it?
- Is the actor teachable?

Directors struggle when faced with a name actor that won't take direction. Not only does the performance lack truthfulness and believability, but it also falls short of the director's vision.

A Great Working Relationship

On one project I have in development, the producer suggested we use Al Pacino as one of the three main characters. After reviewing his work, I realized his performance was either hot or cold, depending on the film. I asked the producer to do some research and we soon learned that when he has a great working relationship with a director his performance is award winning, and when he doesn't have a strong relationship, his work suffers. That was a risk I wasn't willing to take.

Directors know there is a balance between getting an actor's performance to perfectly match his vision and drawing from the creativity that a talent brings to the set. This collaborative process is key to the film's success.

It reminds me of Tom Cruise's collaboration. You will never see Cruise running down steps in an action movie. He learned from several productions early in his career that he looks awkward, not macho, running down steps. Whenever he's in a good collaborative mode with his director, they reposition action to improve his macho look.

Directors keep their eyes open during the screen test for the following:

- Does the actor listen to you?
- Does the actor collaborate well?
- Does the actor accept an atmosphere of open and free exchange?
- Is the actor willing to explore playing what they hint at in a bigger way?
- Is the actor willing to turn overt play into something subtler?
- Do you and the actor work as a team to attain, change, and surpass the expectations you have for the character?

Anything shy of learning the answers to the above 16 questions makes screen tests a complete waste of time. The trend of seeking audition reels is no better than receiving headshots, as none of the above critical questions can be answered by watching a series of clips. It's all about the collaborative process that builds a great relationship between the director and actor.

Dramatic Beat Analysis

There are many components that a director scrutinizes when preparing a scene for production. But the first step is determining the dramatic beats. This term should not be confused with the beats written in dialogue, the pace and rhythm of the story, or the beats in a story's structure. The dramatic beats are those moments in a scene where a character experiences an irreversible change in his thought process or beliefs.

```
EXT - MORNING TEXAS LANDSCAPE - SUNRISE

The DAWN BREAKS on a western landscape. The two men ride their horses
silently, horse hooves CLIP-CLOPPING among the rocks. Django wears
Specks winter coat, with one of Dr.Schultz's white button down dress
shirts underneath it. As they ride through the picturesque scene...
Dr.Schultz breaks the silence./

                    Dr.SCHULTZ
          So, Django, what do you intend to name him?

                    DJANGO
          Who?

                    Dr.SCHULTZ
          Your horse?

                    DJANGO
          What horse?

                    Dr.SCHULTZ
          The horse you're riding.

                    DJANGO
          This ain't my horse./

                    Dr.SCHULTZ
          Yes it is.

                    DJANGO
          No it ain't, it's your horse. I'm just riding
          it.

                    Dr.SCHULTZ
          Well, technically, yes - Wait a minute -/
          technically not. If it's my horse, I can
          give it to you, and as of now, I'm doing such.
          Django, you're now the proud owner of a horse,
          congratulations.

                    DJANGO
          I can't feed no horse. I can't put no horse
          up in no stable.

                    Dr.SCHULTZ
                 (frustrated)
          Don't worry about all that!
```

```
They ride a bit longer in silence...the good doctor composes himself..
then says with a smile;

                         Dr.SCHULTZ
          So....now that that's settled....what do you
          intend to name it? Half the fun of having
          a horse is choosing his name. For instance
          my steed is named Fritz. He's stubborn,
          ornery, and prone to a bad disposition, but I
          couldn't do without him.
                    (he pats Fritz's neck)
          Anyway, the name of one's steed, isn't
          something one does lightly. So once you've
          thought about it for awhile -

                         DJANGO
          - Tony.

                         Dr.SCHULTZ
          - Tony what?

                         DJANGO
          - I dunno, Tony the horse.

                         Dr.SCHULTZ
          Oh, you mean you want to name your horse
          Tony?

                         DJANGO
          Yeah. That's what you jus' asked me, right?

                         Dr.SCHULTZ
          When you're right you're right, indeed I did.
          Why Tony?

                         DJANGO
          I gotta tell ya? You didn't tell me I gotta
          tell ya.

As they continue to converse, they start heading downhill toward a
western town. They pass by a sign that says; "WELCOME TO DAUGHTREY,
TEXAS"

                         Dr.SCHULTZ
          Well I'm naturally curious, of course, but
          there's no reason you MUST tell me. In fact
          an air of mystery adds a dash of panache to
          any steed. And I do believe Tony wears it
          well. Good job Django, well done.
```

A secondary definition comes into play when the beat occurs during the exchange between two characters. These changes are seen more as a shift in power, as each character attempts to achieve or obtain his objective. The character driving the story with dialogue at any given moment is the one in power or controlling the scene, which might rapidly change numerous times within a single scene.

Since "DJANGO" won an Oscar® for Best Original Screenplay, I thought it was best to use one of its scenes as an example. I have marked the beats in the scene with a slash directly after each line that demonstrates the change. The slash is a standard script marking used in the industry for dramatic beats.

Once the director marks the dramatic beats, he can more easily see the patterns, character motivations, and objectives. I'll walk through the basics of the Django scene…

The scene opens with a quiet picturesque setting lightly broken by the clip-clopping of the horse hoofs. Every shot sets the mood and tone of the moment, which is broken by the scene's first beat – Dr. Schultz breaks the silence.

Dr. Schultz owns the conversation until the next beat, when Django says, "This ain't my horse." Django drives the next section of dialogue, until Dr. Schultz has an epiphany and decides to give Django the horse. This settles the argument and brings the tone back to the silence of the scene's opening.

The next beat is Dr. Schultz interrupting the silence again with a litany of dialogue. Django resets the conversation by answering the original question about naming his horse Tony. Django drives the banter, until Dr. Schultz understands the answer and then poses a new question, "Why Tony?"

This gives Dr. Schultz control once again, which allows him to satisfy his reason for starting the conversation. As a result, he is content to bring closure to the chat and return them to their silent ride through the picturesque setting.

These shifts in power within the dialogue make for several clear beats. The beats create significant interest in the minds of the audience, which adds to the film's entertainment value. Without the dramatic beats, the scene would be a boring conversation between two points, rather than an interesting set of dialogue that helps the audience understand the characters.

The Director's Notebook

Director notebooks look significantly different, as they typically reflect their vision and style for a given story. Notebooks can be physically made up of a set of three ring notebooks, a single sketchbook, a diary type book, a digital book, or any combination that allows the director to capture and easily get at his ideas for the film's look and feel.

Notebooks typically hold certain information regardless of the director's taste. Software packages exist that help the director create a digital notebook. Unfortunately, the digital books lack templates or forms for many things that a director needs to capture.

Regardless of style, creativity and inspiration, most directors' notebooks hold information to meet the director's requirements for casting his vision to each department head. Many directors add the department heads' notes and illustrations to their notebooks as they become available.

The notebooks typically include the following sections in no particular order:

Script

(All Department Heads and Principals) Some directors use a master script marked for shooting, while others use a shooting script. Regardless of the markings, it is important for the director to talk through the script with his department heads to transfer his complete artistic vision and notes.

Development or Director Sheets

(Director's Eyes only) This sheet includes any key elements a director may need during the shoot when working with talent. Many directors mark these notes directly on the script rather than having a separate sheet. The content is broken down by scene and includes: Through Line, Motivation, Entrances, Literary Devices, etc. It also includes motivational verbs of varying strengths to help the actors increase or decrease the intensity of their performances.

Beat Sheet

(Director's Eyes only) This sheet includes the breakdown of the story's beats, turning points, emotional charting and story conflicts. These elements help the director to focus on the actors' performances and each character's shift in power.

Character Sheets

(Casting Director) This sheet spells out the key characteristics, age, and other elements necessary for the Casting Director to filter down potential actors for the director's selection.

Character Development Sheets

(Production Designer, Costume Designer, Hair Stylist and Make-Up Artist) This notebook includes descriptions, thumbnail sketches or photos of the director's ideas that reflect the look and feel of each character, including physical stature and appearance, clothing, make-up and hair style.

Action Props & Vehicles Sheets

(Production Designer and Property Master) In this one, descriptions, thumbnail sketches or photos of the director's ideas that reflect the vehicles and props, including how they are used, are found.

Set Design Sheets

(Production Designer, Set Designer and Set Decorator) The notebook will include descriptions, thumbnail sketches and photos of set ideas that reflect the look and feel of the set.

Shot Lists

(Director of Photography) For some directors, the shot list is nothing more than an actual list of shots per scene. Other directors embed their shots into the script using the same markings as the Continuity Supervisor. Most directors add blocking diagrams and set-up cards showing the actor's movement and the camera positions that match the shot list.

Lighting Notes

(Gaffer, Director of Photography and Production Designer) These notes are limited, but give a good sense to the team in advance for altering blue prints or designing set-ups to conform to the imagery and mood of the director's vision.

Physical Effects & Stunt Sheets

(Special Effects Supervisor and Stunt Coordinator) These sheets typically include the visual outcome the director seeks and the story elements, leading up to the moment. This is all discussed in advance in case set alterations or camera equipment are impacted by the functional operation decisions.

Contracts

(Production Manager and Line Producer) Having a set of contracts on hand quickly reduces arguments and helps the director, production manager and 1st AD determine appropriate overtime, if needed.

Script Breakdown

(1st AD, 2nd AD and Production Manager) The Script Breakdown determines workload and helps the team create schedules for cast, crew, vehicles, props, wardrobe, etc.

Location Sheets

(Location Scout and Location Manager) This includes location contracts, contact information, location photos, nearby hotels, etc.

Production Sound

(Sound Mixer) This list covers the ambient and unique sounds required by the story. The more locations sounds captured, the less foley work will be required in post.

Editorial

(Film Editor) While the editor gets the Continuity Supervisor's notes, the director still needs to share his vision for how he sees the story coming together in the Editorial notebook.

Visual Effects Sheet

(Visual Effects Producer/Creative Director) Storyboards tend to fill in these pages to provide discussion on technical requirements in production, including the shooting of background plates and matte work.

Sound/Music Sheets

(Sound Designer) This particular sheet includes a list of critical sounds and music samples that reflect the style and mood the director desires to capture for each scene.

The most productive directors use notebooks to save time and money. Flipping to a certain page is much faster than trying to remember all the details of every scene. Some directors use the notebook only during prep time the night before a shoot or when in meetings with department heads, while others keep it with them on the set for last second decisions. In either case, the notebook is the production bible for the film.

Camera Set-Ups and Shot Lists

Determining the camera set-ups for the day and its relevant shot list is important in order to make sure everything is captured and the team moves in the most logical and speedy order. Unfortunately, most independent filmmakers fly by the seat of their pants instead of preplanning. This causes them to lose numerous hours in shooting time over the duration of a feature film.

Camera set-ups can be drawn on a 3X5 card, or created in an iPad app – I've done both. If the scene requires a lot of movement, I prefer the iPad app so I can demonstrate the camera movement and actor blocking through animation.

The set-up cards are always an aerial view and display camera position and any dolly tracks. They also include characters, extras and the floor plan, and sometimes action props. The cards show all elements, include starting and ending positions. Depending on the software app or the amount of room on the paper, the lighting set-up may be added as well.

Arrows and lines are typically used to show camera and actor movement. The shape of the camera movement line reveals if it uses a track or handheld/steadicam shot. Track is always straight or precisely curved, while handheld/steadicam lines move in any shape or follow any contour.

Every camera must be labeled in some fashion that carries over to the shot list. When I use the iPad app, I export the camera information to an excel spreadsheet in the form of a shot list, which takes less than 5 seconds. When I use 3X5 cards, I typically put the shot list on the back of the card or on a second card.

The shot list includes the camera name, the shot type, the lens, camera equipment like dollies or cranes, and any movement, focus or zooming instructions. My experience allows me to rough out the list prior to meeting with the director of photography. Since his expertise is invaluable, I review and update the information as I present my logic for the emotional imagery I need for the scene.

No matter how much I prep during development or pre-production, there are always changes the morning of the shoot, not to mention during creative moments with the actors as we explore variations of the scene. The best way to keep these changes organized is to number every known shot in advance, using a numbering system that readily accepts updates and changes.

The numbering system I use gives the DP, editor, script supervisor and me an immediate visual understanding of what scene it is from, its shot type and what character it includes. This makes searches quick both manually and online. It also helps the editing team prep the clips for the editor.

By prepping the camera set-ups in advance, the director can save the team a tremendous amount of time during the shoot. It also gives a great foundation for those creative changes that happen on the fly. This allows a more organized freedom that helps the editorial team, rather than the wild creative activities that force the editorial team to suffer through extremely long days.

Finding the Action for Actors

Motion pictures have always been about action. If it were not so, they would have been called "still" pictures. Movement makes film what it is and we find numerous techniques developed over the years that take advantage of the medium. Between all the techniques used in chase scenes to move a story forward, dolly and tracking shots to heighten dialogue, or even steadicam shots for continuous shooting, one thing stands out: Actors need action.

I've had opportunity to work with two kinds of actors: seasoned professionals and amateurs. Regardless of which camp they live in, the most important job a director has is to make them feel at home within their character – bolstering their self-esteem to the point where being something they're not, doesn't intimidate them.

Unfortunately, in the independent world, there are more bad scripts than good ones. Poorly worded scripts can cut at the very fabric of encouraging the actor to his best performance. One example of how bad it can get stated:

```
TERRANCE leaves with a surly expression.

                      TERRANCE
           You are a fool.

He steps through the door.
```

While I can picture the shot with the guy leaving in a gruff fashion, I can't fathom how the actor can play "surly". Nor can I understand how a rookie director might attempt to get him to play "more" surly. If I were an actor listening to the director tell me to be "more surly", I'm not sure what I could do to facilitate that request. Nor would I know what I had done to be surly in the first place, making me terribly self-conscious in that moment.

Actors can't play surly because it is not an action.

Webster states that the definition of surly is: irritably sullen and churlish in mood or manner. There is no actor on this earth that can "play" anything from within the definition. And yes, I put the word play in quote marks because it suggests "action."

Actors need actions – Verbs. Not adjectives. Just verbs.

It's the job of every actor to research his or her lines and determine what actions are suggested within the script. The above line from the script gives a hint at it, but only the director knows which path should be followed. The director owns the creative outcome of the picture and must give direction to the actor in order to focus in on one of a myriad of possibilities.

In this case, I'll choose to direct the script line by suggesting to the actor that he is motivated:

- to rebuke
- to berate
- to reprimand

By giving three verbs as examples, the actor is able to get a good sense of what I'm looking for. However, sometimes I'll give one example at a time and see how it plays out. If I need more of something, I try a stronger verb, if less, a softer verb. The key is making sure it's always a verb that can be acted out.

To rebuke, berate or reprimand someone requires some form of action. A softer word choice might be to scoff. A harder version might be to shame. In all cases, the verbs generate a movement or action that most actors know how to play.

For instance, the actor might turn back as he walks out the door and state his line while leaning forward with a glint in his eye. Another actor, depending on what he brings to the character, might choose to arrogantly spout his words to bring shame down on the other character. Still, another might turn with an intensity in his voice and move toward the other character spitting out each word, then turn as if nothing happened and walk away.

Telling an actor to be surly, or worse yet, how to be surly, forces the actor to play the role mechanically, which shows up in the film. By using great verbs, the actor's creative juices flow and they are able to draw from experience and play the scene naturally. When the director sees the natural response, if it is not quite what he wants, he can't say to give it more without making the performance mechanical. Instead, he must find a stronger verb to inspire more intensity.

Since the actor can't see that their performance is at the right level of intensity, he must trust the director to have his best interest and performance at heart. After all, being too intense for the scene makes it look way over the top and possibly to the point of being silly. And, too little might mean the death of the scene or a lethargic character, which lacks appeal or drama.

This director and actor relationship is sensitive and requires both people to participate in the character's development. The director must do everything in his power to draw out the best performance and protect the actor from looking mechanical or out of place for the scene. Mean while the actor must keep his character fresh and consistent with all other discussions and scripted scenes.

Together, the relationship builds award-winning performances that will be remembered beyond a lifetime. This is all made possible by a handful of verbs being used in place of adjectives. And, with the decentralization of Hollywood, the independents that can develop great action will see greater box office success going forward.

Driving the Character with a Secret

One screenplay I worked on was with a producer whose list of credits included Nickelodeon and Disney. We teamed up to write a love story that was bookended by a courtroom drama. The story required some very intense scenes and humorous relief to keep the audience focused on how the story ended. And yes, the boy got the girl. But the "how" was unique.

The three main characters drove the story. The dual protagonists were strong-willed and the antagonist had a deep secret that drove his passion throughout the film. This hidden secret was the fuel for many intense scenes and quirky moments.

To strengthen weaker scenes, actors typically employ the concept of withholding a secret from their peers. The use of a secret gives the mind additional angles to consider during a particular scene and visually creates depth of character from the camera's point of view. The subtle facial changes from merely thinking of the secret are actually picked up by the camera. And, since the audience doesn't know the secret, it reads like there is more to the character than meets the eye.

Cameras have always been able to detect what is real, and separate it from what is fake or make believe. That's why actors work so hard to find common ground with their character and play the scenes as honestly as possible.

During a chat with Catherine Hicks, known for *7th Heaven* and *Star Trek IV: The Voyage Home,* she shared that during the shooting of *Game Time: Tackling the Past,* she drew from a time when her own daughter was in the hospital. This fueled her role of an anxious wife in a waiting room, hoping for good news. The use of this technique or secret brought more depth to her character and created an honest scene for the camera.

Some of the best screenplays infer something unknown in the character's background that fuels the performance and passion of the actors. This passion or edgy unknown causes the audiences' minds to fill in the gaps based on their own experiences. That imaginative exercise strengthens their bond to the character. Once that bond is achieved, the audience feels compelled to watch the remainder of the film to understand the character's outcome.

In the case of my recent script, the person with the greatest amount of integrity carries the greatest secret. The character seems too good to be true until the secret is revealed. Interestingly enough, once the reveal hits, the audience trusts the character all the more, since she has overcome her life's obstacle and had everything turn out for her good in the end.

12 Essentials of Directing Actors

In watching and chatting with numerous actors and directors over the years, I've learned a few things that directors do well and not so well. During this time span, ideals have changed within the production world, so my focus will be on those key points directors use to encourage actors to deliver a truthful performance.

Take An Acting Class

Actors are vulnerable and sensitive people that need an encouraging and understanding director. The best way for directors to inspire great performances is form them to understand the acting process. To keep up with the latest trends, directors should take acting or improvisational classes every so often.

Make A Connection

An actor's job is intense and exposed, which can cause him or her to feel overly sensitive or vulnerable. The director needs to come alongside, as a trusted advisor. Actors rarely need to be challenged or have an authority figure bear down on them. Most are artists that critique or compare themselves to others to their own detriment.

Kill Critical Speak

The director owns the set and must stop any cast or crew from saying anything negative to actors. Direction must come only from the director, who fully understands the overall vision and can give proper and affirming recognition. If anyone on the set feels a need to make suggestions or confer with the director about someone's performance, it must be done in private, if at all. The director must protect the actors.

Ask Questions

The last thing an actor needs on set is a director that is authoritarian or overbearing as he bellows out commands or instructions. Each actor is an expert at her character and because the director is focused on everything, the professional actor will maintain that expert status.

It's therefore prudent for the director to change the actor's performance inductively, by asking questions. By drawing the actor into the thinking process, she is able to discover for herself what the character needs to do. This activity strengthens the actor's ownership of the character and enhances her performance.

Treat Actors Equally

An actor's emotions can take its toll throughout the shooting day. Great directors try to keep an eye on each actor's emotional status and take specific time to remind her that she is liked and respected. The director is a powerful leader that should share this treatment equally with all actors to maintain a mutually warm environment in which the actors can safely perform. Leaving an actor out of this personalized attention can send her reeling out of control.

Be Courteous

Directors can raise the performance bar by being courteous and avoiding the common mistake of telling an actor how she failed in a performance. By saying, "What was that? You can't bellow out your lines. Let's do another take and give me less," the director increases the actor's fear and stiffens her next take.

Instead, a director might consider saying, "I'd like to try something a little different on this next take. I wonder if you could maintain your emotional intensity and drench the other character with a dangerous calm." This gives the actor more to work with and inspires creativity and performance.

Avoid Common Acting Problems

Acting is self-conscious and self-judgmental, which many times can cause an actor to act from her head, instead of her heart. The director must work with the actor to make sure she is focused on the character and not herself. This approach will avoid numerous problems that typically arise during any given shooting day, and help to draw out an honest or truthful performance.

Promote Relaxation And Focus

Relaxation is important to making sure the actor doesn't project her voice as if on a stage. Relaxation will also impact the way in which she carries herself. When a scene calls for tension, it will naturally grow from the relaxed state to appear in her hands, walk, voice and face. Any time anxiety creeps in, the actor will become stilted in her performance. A director can improve the performance by reminding the actor of what she's done well. Even redirecting her focus off her feelings and back onto the character will reduce any temporary lack in confidence.

Clarify Subtext

Reviewing subtext during rehearsal will help an actor focus on each line, glance or action. Every element of her performance must lead to her character's super objective, and remind her for what she is fighting., The subtext can be clarified with a verb to be played, a character to which she plays, and an intended effect her character wants as the outcome.

Kill Anticipation

It is difficult for a director to have an actor play a part "naturally" in a specific way, as the mere mention of "doing it naturally" makes the performance stilted. Within that moment, the actor gets trapped in her head and starts to anticipate a line or action. She might also purposely hold back in an attempt to be more natural, which creates an awkward lag and reveals the actor has repeated that moment several times before in rehearsal.

One of the best ways to avoid this conundrum is to walk the actor through the character's thinking process, while salting in moment-by-moment clues as the performance unfolds – just like it happens in real life.

Kill Indicating

It's common for an actor to increase the visible size of her performance in hopes of reaching the audience or allowing them to see her character's personality. Unfortunately, the camera lens is only kind to subtle performance and the actor finds herself overworking and destroying her character in the process.

Having the actor think about a secret or some internal struggle during the performance allows the audience to see that there is more depth to the character without presenting an over-the-top performance. Directing the actor as if speaking to her character can also effectively generate the desired subtle secrecy effect.

Speak In Verbs

Many actors memorize certain actions to help them "do business" during their scenes. Those actions can weaken their performances because they often do not flow naturally from the character. Instead of having an actor pull something out of her bag of tricks, the director can share verbs that stimulate creative ideas, developing new actions based solely on the character. An example might come from a script line such as, "She keeps up with her, dodging in and out of shadows."

The immediate thought an actor might come up with in response is moving from tree to tree. peering around, trying to keep up with the other character. However, the director can bring to bear an arsenal of variations on the movement by asking the actor to "trail" the other characters. Or, he can step up the intensity by using words such as: follow, track, pursue, hunt, stalk, or chase. Each verb intensifies the action and sets a new mental picture for the actor to perform.

If I were to add a "don't" to the list for amateur directors, I'd have to recommend not ever demonstrating how you'd like something played. This act instantly reduces the director's credibility to zero, and the actor will not be able to deliver the performance the director envisioned This is not to take away from the director showing an actor her blocking, as he walks the actor down the path, discussing the character's motivation.

The key for directors is to remember that the actor is an expert at her character while the director is more concerned with the picture as a whole The director will know what works and what doesn't, and must use questions to guide the actor in creating performance variations until the director gets what will work best on screen – something the actor will need to trust the director to accomplish.

The ABC's of Actor Set Etiquette

Every set is run with different guidelines, but there is an overall etiquette that fits most acting situations. The following "On Set Rules" can be used if the production team doesn't provide their own guidelines:

ALWAYS BE ALERT: Energy levels must stay high on the set. Stay alert to where the camera is and how movement is blocked. Keeping an energy bar nearby might help give that extra needed boost after hours of hard work, especially if the day lengthens into overtime.

BE COURTEOUS: The entertainment industry is made up of a small group of people that will eventually know each other. The odds of working with someone on another project within seven years are high. Treating everyone professionally and courteously will go a long way to help capture the next job.

CHECK IN AND OUT: Always check in and out with the proper person at any set or location. If an actor needs to step away to a restroom, he or she needs to let the proper person know. And actors should remember to hand in vouchers at the end of each day.

DON'T CHEW GUM: This one shouldn't require any explanation for actors. Besides, don't we all know the myriad of things that can go wrong with gum on a set?

ENTOURAGE STAYS AT HOME: Do not bring friends or family to the set. Leave cameras, drugs and alcohol at home.

Keep cell phones off, except in appointed areas during appointed times.

FANS ARE UNWELCOME: Talking to the star or director is taboo unless he or she speaks first. Do not ask them for a photo opportunity, autograph or anything else that might break their concentration. This rule tends to slide during lunch break, unless the star or director is in a meeting.

GIVING NOTES IS FOOLISH: This is another sure way to get fired. Telling someone how to improve their performance or clarifying how they messed up is grounds for being fired on the spot. No one has the right to suggest anything different than what the director shared with or artistically required of his actors.

HIERARCHY IS WORTH LISTENING TO: Knowing the hierarchy of a show is critical to know whom to listen and who overrides whom. The producer trumps everyone, unless there are multiple producers. Typically a director that also carries a producer's title is above everyone on the set.

ISSUES TO AVOID: Actors should not argue about what is not in his or her control. The fastest way to get fired from a set is to argue about something required by the hierarchy. Actors should take time to know who is over him or her and be ready to answer "Yes."

JOKES AND PRANKS: There is always a certain level of joking to keep a set atmosphere conducive to play. Unfortunately, the person who takes it too far typically gets fired.

KEEP HANDS OFF: Do not touch any equipment that you have not been authorized to touch. This includes props, grip equipment, working set pieces, etc.

LATE IS A FOUR-LETTER WORD: The industry norm is that being on time to set is considered being late. Ms. Manners would add that "late" is a four-letter word worth avoiding. Most actors arrive 15-30 minutes early.

MONEY TALK IS OFF LIMITS: No one likes to hear about the money for which an actor was contracted, especially if it is significantly higher than everyone else's. Money issues can sour any positive atmosphere on set and the topic is off limits.

NETWORK DURING FREE TIME: Sets are great places to network, especially since about 75 percent of all jobs come by word of mouth from someone on set. However, it is critical to restrict networking to meals or free times. Don't ever allow a future work opportunity to sabotage a current project.

OBSERVE CHARACTERS: Paying attention to what other actors are doing with their characters helps tweak one's character to the same style and reality the director is creating. It also allows the actor to play off others more realistically.

PRACTICE INTERNALLY: Just as baseball players mentally review their next steps based on strategic conditions, an actor should mentally review his or her next actions based on how the scene is being directed. This will help the actor repeat certain movements. should the director call for another take.

QUIET ON SET: The set is a professional work zone that costs thousands of dollars an hour to operate. The only people talking should be those with lines or the production hierarchy / department heads. Any conversation can create costly delays. If the average person on set makes a $1 per minute, and there are 100 people on set, a quick 3 minute question and answer could cost the producer $300 plus rental equipment and other set costs. There are proper times to ask questions of the right people.

RECEIVE NOTES PROFESSIONALLY: When the director or his staff gives a note, accept it professionally and trust that he understands the big picture and how everything artistically melds together.

SPILLS ON COSTUMES ARE UNCOOL: Bringing a nonspillable water bottle is a good practice. Using a smock for lunchtime may be the only solution if actors can't change before eating.

TRANSPORTATION GUIDELINES: A driver can be a best friend on location sets. They work hard to get actors to locations on time and get little credit for it. Taking time to be polite and thanking the driver will make a world of difference on those days when something goes wrong.

UNSAFE CONDITIONS: Sets are normally built for temporary use and easy tear down. This sometimes results in jagged edges or chipping floorboard edges, which can easily cause twisted ankles. Report any size of danger or potential issues immediately. The last thing the producer wants is a liability on set that could cost the show.

VEXING NOT ALLOWED: Some actors try to overshadow or upstage others, but often learn what it is like to be fired. There is a tendency to be drawn into the game and overplay a role to compensate for how another actor changed a shot. Being a consummate professional requires the actor trust that the director, AD's or PA's are watching, and will eventually yank the problem actor from the set.

WAIT PATIENTLY: Hurry up and wait has been the slogan on set for over 100 years. Actors must be patient and learn to keep themselves mentally active when on hold for long periods. Be willing to hurry when asked and patient when waiting.

XEROX® IS TRADEMARKED: Professional actors talk about photocopies, not a Xerox®. They talk about facial tissue, not a Kleenex®. The industry is filled with lawsuits protecting copyrights, trademarks and patents. The last thing an actor needs is to unintentionally get drawn into a lawsuit because he or she said the wrong thing to the press. Learn from the appropriate people what should and shouldn't be said during on set interviews.

YACKING IS TABOO: The set is no place for a sick person. If you have a bad cold or anything contagious, stay away. The professional response is to call the appropriate person early so they have time to find a replacement. Those that show up to the set sick will be sent home and considered unprofessional.

ZONE IN TO ROLE: Be in character and in the moment. Everything an actor trains and works for makes each performance moment excellent. Losing focus can diminish all the hard work in a matter of seconds. Be professional and keep focused.

Having been behind the scenes many times, I can tell you productive sets are ones that embrace the above common forms of set etiquette. Actors that embrace these principles will rise to the top. No one likes to work with an actor that lacks proper set etiquette.

Using a Director Viewfinder

I was on the set of an independent feature film and realized the one thing slowing down their production was an indecisive director that lacked a director viewfinder. Instead of the director quickly determining what type of shot set-up and lens he wanted using the glass, he made the camera and grip team move the equipment around two to three times to determine each set-up. That choice cost them 45 minutes of shooting during the time of my visit.

The experience prompted me to provide five reasons why independent filmmakers should use a director viewfinder:

Preproduction

Many directors create a shot list and map out their camera set-ups during preproduction. Some use small objects to represent their talent and test their blocking with set prints, models, or taped tabletops. By using the director viewfinder in this way, the director can estimate the approximate camera position for the DP prior to the shoot.

Location Scouting

Few independent productions have the benefit of a location scout. By keeping a director viewfinder handy, the filmmaker can immediately test the composition of any cinematic location he stumbles upon.

Develop DP Short Cuts

The director viewfinder can be set to any standard aspect ratios (Academy, TV-4X3, 1.66, 1.76-16X9, 1.85, 2.35, and 2.55) and formats (Film: S16, 35mm, Anamorphic and Video: 2/3", 1/2", 1/3", Mini DV, 1/4", 1/5", 1/6"), so when the director finds his shot, he can immediately share the specifications of the shot with the DP by looking at the settings. This allows the DP to quickly delegate important information to his camera and grip teams.

Simplify Grips Job

Film shoots can require multiple cameras, dollies, cranes, jib arms, etc. Having the grips set and shifted each set-up until it's close to the director's vision tires the team and slows down the shoot. Ideally the equipment would only move once per set-up, which is easily facilitated by a director using his viewfinder.

Prepare For A Studio Picture

Directors need to build skills and good habits that create productive conditions during a shoot. A director that burns $50-$500 an hour on a small production is typically more wasteful than a director working a studio picture, who uses a director viewfinder and burns through $5K-$50K per hour. He typically has a process or methodology that provides a highly creative and efficient environment.

Everyone knows that a writer must have software to properly write screenplays, but few understand the critical importance of the director viewfinder, as well as the director notebook. The viewfinder allows the director to pre-visualize the limits he places on the audience and allows his first step in translating the written word from the screenplay to a visual for the silver screen.

By carefully selecting the right series of images, the director is able to move the audience emotionally down the path of his choice. He is able to determine what they see and when they see it, making them vulnerable to his dramatic story. To that end, I started using a director viewfinder with my first directing job and found it to be a tool I couldn't live without.

I have the Alan Gordon Mark IV director viewfinder (The latest version is the MarkVb) and the Opteka mini director viewfinder. While the glass is better on the Mark IV, the mini has the latest formats and aspect ratios. The mini is convenient to carry in my pocket when I don't have my backpack handy. Prices range from $99 – $700+, depending on the features desired.

Directing the Action and Theme

Most directors that I've met can quickly tell you how to direct an action sequence, but few can elaborate on developing the subtle nuances of the theme. Thankfully, 70 to 80 percent of a movie is driven by the action plot line and most writers create a theme that finds its way to the surface regardless of the director's experience level. There is, however, a significant difference between great films and the not-so-great, which can be attributed to directors that strengthen their stories by nurturing their themes.

I recently read about a wedding party where the host miscalculated the number of guests and the amount of wine they would drink. The party was about to see an embarrassed host, but thankfully a hero quietly arrived in the background. Once requested, he told the servants to fill the five empty ceremonial vases with water, dip a cup into one, and take it to the head server.

The head server tasted a sample from the wine batch and was startled. He made a big deal of the great-tasting wine because the culture always switched out the great wine for some two-buck chuck after everyone was tipsy, figuring that no one would notice. But, this host held back the best for last, which was worthy of praise. The crowd loved it and the host was held in high esteem.

Aside from the mysterious miracle performed by the hero, the story has a great subplot that carries a strong theme. It's about a hero coming to the aid of someone in need. Not someone who lost his house in a flood, or barely survived a bloodcurdling car wreck, but someone who was about to be embarrassed based on his own shortsightedness. The hero had a great deal of empathy and was very diplomatic on behalf of the host.

The hero didn't grandstand and perform the miracle for everyone to see, which would have put him in a great place in the public eye and devastate the host that had botched up. But instead, the hero kept everything low-key and allowed the host to take the credit. In other words, the hero was more concerned about the emotional well-being of the host than meeting the needs of the crowd. We learn that the hero is very personable and interested in the little things in life — a great role model.

When a director focuses on the action to the detriment of the theme, he misses some of the most important life changing moments that can give the audience a reason to contemplate the movie time and time again. By focusing on the theme, a director can bring the humanity of the film to life. Without it, the film is left only with the fun factor and visual energy of the story, which can actually grow stale.

Have you ever gone to a movie that was really well made, but didn't compel you to think about anything or inspire you to take some form of action? Directors that lose sight of their theme or allow it to be overshadowed by gimmicks and effects in order to bring in larger audiences typically helm that type of movie. It's important to note that only theme-enriched films plant the seed of life-changing ideas in the audiences' minds, giving them food for thought and a desire to watch the movie again.

Directing Intensity

A director recently asked me how he could improve his intense scenes with less-experienced actors. I told him the key to the level of intensity is in the actor's perception concerning how he is coming across on screen. Most feel like their intensity isn't big enough unless they become theatrical, which doesn't work on camera.

The best way to help the actor understand his level of intensity is by painting a picture in his mind of what big intensity would look like and then ask him to think about it during the scene, but not portray it. This creates internal conflict and an intensity begging to come out, which reads very well on camera.

Telling the actor to bring more or less to his performance is a waste of time. Whenever we tell the actor to back off a bit on the intensity, he has no point of reference and feels awkward, which detracts from the scene. Instead, telling the actor to picture himself in another situation and express what his character is fighting for in a way that he can pre visualize will help immensely.

Once you can tell the actors have the picture in mind, you can return them to thinking about it, but not acting on it. This will generate enough internal conflict to build intensity from the camera's viewpoint. However, you will frustrate the actors and must compensate by encouraging them after each take. Without doing so, the actors will start withdrawing and alter their characters. After all, it takes a lot of confidence to play something other than what they are.

When helping the actor to develop what the character is fighting for, it's important to use action words. Saying that he is shuffling toward his destiny, or raging against a bureaucracy designed to hold back the little people, gives the actor something specific from which to work.

"Shuffling" and "raging" are both words that describe a visualization of an emotion and are ideal for building character. All trained actors are taught to "do business," and using action-based words adds to that skill. It helps actors turn the emotional elements of their characters into action or reactions, which then feeds intensity.

I can't help but notice that the vast majority of acting awards have gone to actors that had good directors. Rarely will you find an actor achieve excellence with a poor director. The reason is simple, actors can't see their performances and they can't come up with all the needed visualizations of their emotions.

It takes a great director to create a visual moment that is safe for an actor to dig deep down inside, and draw out strong emotional ties from their own lives that are action-oriented. Few actors will trust their deep emotions with a director that doesn't know how to visualize those emotions, or make them come across well on camera.

Imagine how an actor would feel as he draws from a point of vulnerability to find that the director allowed the intensity to appear over –the-top, making the actor look foolish. The actor would feel burnt and during his next opportunity would perform what is safe, rather than award-winning. The director owns the emotional tone of the picture and the artistic expression. Therefore, directors must work to build trust with the actors.

I worked with one actor a couple years ago who, in my opinion, was one of the best stage actors in the area. However, the camera is far more sensitive to action than the stage, and everything must be played smaller. During his first shot, I watched a stage performance. He could sense that it was over the top and too animated for the camera and asked for help.

I had the choice of saying play it smaller, as most directors would do, but I didn't. I told him that his character was headed to an appointment with a fragile piece of art to exchange for a $50,000 bonus check. Then I asked him to do a dry run without "acting," but to think about the fragile art and his bonus check. The intensity of his care for the fragile - coupled with a sense of speed - read well on camera. The camera saw a concerned man, moving quickly to resolve.

I had the camera team roll with the idea that we'd use a tail slate if it worked. The performance was perfect. His stage presence disappeared without undermining his emotions. He was able to keep his stage-thinking in place, along with his confidence. The scene worked beautifully. His next shot was even better after having shot such a successful take.

A director that can protect his actor's emotions during each take will draw out the perfect level of intensity, giving the actor a great piece for his or her reel, not to mention festival accolades.

The key is helping the actor draw from and visualize his life experiences and emotions.

For those working with experienced professionals, selecting key action verbs to describe the characters' objectives or what they are fighting for will more quickly accomplish the same result. Learning about actors' emotional reserves and their abilities to translate them to the screen will help the director decide which approach will work best.

Forget the Master Scene

Master filmmakers have been touting the importance of shooting a master scene for decades, but in today's visual society it is no longer necessary. Now that we're in the third generation of film viewers, the audience has learned how to read films and no longer need things to be explained to them. The 1977 release of Star Wars demonstrated that proof with its use of time compression and fast cuts.

Prior to Star Wars, a scene might unfold like this:

A car stops alongside of a curb in a residential area. The key turns off and is removed from the steering column. The car door opens and a reporter steps out. He reaches back into the car for a pen and notebook. The reporter closes the door and locks it. Walking around the car, he moves up the sidewalk toward the house. His winged-tip shoes move quickly up the staircase. He pushes the doorbell. The reporter readies his notebook and pen. The door slowly opens, revealing a nervous woman that doesn't want her story published.

After Star Wars, the same scene might unfold like this:

A car stops alongside of a curb in a residential area. The doorbell ring echoes within the house, as a nervous woman opens the door to find a reporter standing with pen and paper in hand.

Both presentations get across the important story elements of a reporter after a story and a nervous woman who doesn't want it published. The first one was typically shot as a master scene and then reshot with potential close-ups, over the shoulder shots, and other types of shots that might include a crane or dolly. This type of shooting would require a good four hours to rehearse and shoot on location.

Today, the scene would open with a moving crane shot of the car parking along the curb. The interior shot might use a dolly to follow the woman to the door and a jib arm might move it into an over the shoulder shot as the door opens to reveal the reporter. The exterior shot would be filmed within an hour by the second unit team, which would keep costs down. The interior would be shot on the sound stage in less than an hour.

The cost of creating the master scene is high for independent budgets and its benefits are no longer relevant for today's filmmakers. The odds of more than four seconds of a master shot being used is slim; let alone using it in its entirety. If the scene is really long, there might be reason to use a master shot to break the scene in two, but most of the time filmmakers will only use the first or last three or four seconds of the shot – making the remainder a very costly unusable piece of film.

Today's directors plan ahead for the visual and emotional impact they want their audiences to receive. The director requires only the shots that truly move the story forward and the rest are no longer filmed, thanks to an audience that can now read a series of images as a story. This new ability of the mind filling in the visual gaps will soon make film the most prolific story telling device for years to come.

The only remaining reason for a master shot is to cover for an unprepared director or one that isn't able to visualize the film in his head. The master scene would capture how the actor plays out the scene in order for the director to figure out what camera angles and shots he might need to tell the story. Today, however, storyboards, animatics and previs (previsualization) can easily replace this technique, while saving a significant amount of money and time.

Managing a Locked Script

Have you ever regretted locking a script, because an hour later you had revisions? You no longer have to regret it, as long as you know the rules to manage the most current version of the screenplay. And the good news is that the rules are standardized within the production community. However, the rules do change a bit from the United States, to England, to India, to China, to Australia, etc.

Colored Paper

The original locked script is published on white paper. Any changes to a script page are distributed on colored paper. There is a hierarchy of colors so everyone knows what order of change they have received. The paper colors are in the below order:

- White
- Blue
- Pink
- Yellow
- Green
- Goldenrod
- Buff
- Salmon
- Cherry
- Tan

Should a script have more changes after the color tan is used, the colors start again from the top.

The color pattern is helpful during a production that sees many changes. For instance, if the production manager couldn't find you with last night's changes and hands you a yellow script page, you would know to pitch it if the director handed you a green page after his brilliant ideas developed during breakfast.

Revision Marks

Once the script is in everyone's hands, all revisions need to be marked. The revision mark is in the right margin and typically set at 7.8" from the left edge of the paper. The most common mark is the asterisk.

If a scene is replaced with one or two other scenes, then the revision is noted. In the below example, scene 72 was omitted, and then replaced with two new scenes marked by a letter to convey order.

```
72     OMITTED

72A    INT. CELLAR – NIGHT

       The lamp cord dangles over the Zombie.

72B    EXT. BARN – CONTINUOUS

       The farmer grabs a special zombie-killing
       pitchfork.

73     EXT. CELLAR – CONTINUOUS

       The farmer breaks the lock off of the
       cellar door.
```

If a series of scenes are omitted the script would read as follows:

```
72    OMITTED
thru
72B

73    EXT. CELLAR – CONTINUOUS

      The farmer breaks the lock off of the
      cellar door.
```

If a scene or two need to be squeezed into a script, the scene number would have an A or B added to it, like below:

```
78    INT. BUS – DAY

      Isabella abruptly turns from Josh and
      looks out the window.

78A   EXT. PARKING LOT – CONTINUOUS

      Isabella steps down from the bus and keeps
      walking.

78B   INT. BUS – CONTINUOUS

      Josh grabs his mangled flower bouquet and
      heads to the door.

79    EXT. TRAIN STATION – CONTINUOUS

      Josh hands Isabella a bouquet of flowers.
```

Should another scene idea pop into the writer's head that must be located between 78A and 78B, a letter would precede the number.

```
78A   EXT. PARKING LOT – CONTINUOUS

      Isabella steps down from the bus and keeps
      walking.

A78B  INT. TICKET BOOTH – CONTINUOUS

      The Conductor glances out the window at a
      woman walking alone.
```

```
78B   INT. BUS – CONTINUOUS

      Josh grabs his mangled flower bouquet and
      heads to the door.
```

If a lot of the page is deleted within a locked script, it will remain short or mostly blank. If a lot of scenes are added, then an extra page would be added and marked with a letter after the page number. This means that page 51 would have a page 51A added to it.

Once 50% of the script is changed, the writer typically replaces it with a new draft on all white papers with no asterisks.

Establishing a Production Workflow

Whether operating in the corporate work force, being a stay-at-home mom, or directing a multi-million dollar picture, everyone accomplishes more in the morning than in the afternoon. That is unless they sleep through most of their morning. This common practice must be considered when developing a production workflow.

Setting the workflow for a picture is critical for meeting the deadline and staying on schedule. The key factors that directors and first assistant directors face in developing their workflow include:

1. Production crews get more work done in the morning than after lunch. Therefore directing the scenes with higher difficulty levels or more creative challenges can take advantage of the morning crew, while simple set ups are best in the afternoon.

2. Moving a production team between locations is time-consuming and costly. The director and production manager will take this into account and not require more than one move a day. If multiple locations are required, efficiencies and cost savings can be gained from a second crew by moving only the director and actors.

3. Selecting when the first shot is to take place and sticking with the schedule are huge factors in meeting daily deadlines. The first assistant director can help keep the cast and crew on schedule by keeping him in the loop, especially if he is directing the background.

4. Setting milestones within the day for creative shots and difficult scenes are critical to staying on budget. Since there are typically only six hours from start to lunch, it is crucial the director hits his morning milestones and explores only creative concepts within the additional time frame earned by finishing earlier than originally planned.

By keeping up to pace in the above manner, the director will find the producer hanging over his shoulder far less often. He will be freed up for more creative thought and the extra time gained from these disciplines will allow him to help the actors explore other aspects of their characters, which will strengthen several scenes and the overall film.

The Production Trinity

Great films start with great writing, but the trinity formed by the director, director of photography, and the production designer creates high production values, giving rise to excellence. Without the trinity, films can't surpass the quality of an average B movie.

Cost-cutting methods used by many independent films include the merging of the director and the DP into one person, leaving out the production designer all together. While a few films lacking a trinity have been remarkable, most can't compete in the marketplace. This is due to the low production values and shortcuts that occur because there isn't enough manpower.

When a creative trinity is part of a production, the focus on detail plays out in the following three ways:

Director

The director owns the vision for the film and needs to have a strong opinion on what the film will be. He is responsible for how the story is told visually with a specific point of view. He must have a strong sense about how to translate the written word (screenplay) to the screen cinematically.

The director's focus covers the story, characters, motivation, technical and aesthetics -- the overall look and feel of the film. His point of view will determine how the tools of the trade are applied to the story. He also collaborates with the department heads and makes all final decisions on design and photographic elements.

Production Designer

Being the head of the Art Department, the designer is in charge of the physical environments including the creation, construction and selection of sets and locations. He also oversees the costume designer, wardrobe, hair and make-up.

His team focuses on the period, space, texture and colors. In pre-production, he collaborates with the director to understand his impression of the story and how he will pull it together.

Director of Photography

The DP or Cinematographer is responsible to capture the director's vision on film/video. His collaboration with the director and production designer is for the purpose of creating the look and visual style of the film that best serves the director's vision.

He oversees a team that covers the camera, composition, lighting, and movement. The choice of equipment, lenses, processes, and digital enhancements determine the perspective, color and visual texture of the story.

The trinity sometimes uses previs -- a tool/technique to pre-visualize scenes -- to make sure they clearly understand the same visual story elements. Some trinities use software for pre-visualization, while others use storyboards or animatics, and still others use models and miniatures.

When the right combination of artists forms a trinity, the audience generates award ceremony buzz and box office sales.

The First Assistant Director is a Must

I have directed shows with a first Assistant Director (known as an AD) and without one. I can tell you the difference in how the sets were run and how much of my time was focused on the actors instead of the petty problems that surface during a shoot. The best thing about having a 1st AD on a film is the amount of director's time freed up to focus on bringing a story to life.

It shouldn't be a surprise that out of all the national and international productions I've directed, only those pictures with a 1st AD won major awards for "Best Director." The first time I noticed this pattern was at the U.S. and International Film and Video Festival where I was competing against thousands of directors. The ability of each director was high and the only difference between the top ten were subtle nuances that required a 100 percent focus on his craft.

A good 1st AD is extremely valuable to a director and his creative process. It frees him up to work more closely with the actors, bringing such depth to their characters that the audience is compelled to watch the movie again. This freedom also gives the director more time to develop his shot list with the DP, focusing on the cinematic vision that drives the emotional beats within the story.

Some of the key responsibilities managed by the 1st AD are below:

- Run the set.
- Develop the script breakdown.
- Work with the director on the shooting schedule.

- Manage the schedule.
- Coordinate production activities.
- Manage the 2nd and 3rd ADs and oversee the Runners/PAs.
- Oversee the blocking of atmosphere.
- Be the liaison with the production office.
- Be the link between the director and the cast & crew.
- Oversee the publishing of the production reports.
- Oversee the acquisition of locations, props, and equipment.
- Oversee the development of previs or storyboards.
- Keep up to date on the weather reports.
- Manage set/location discipline.
- Work within budget limitations.

The qualities or skills of a great 1st AD are:

- Diplomatic
- Authoritative
- Approachable
- Organized
- Time efficient.
- Aware of potential trouble
- Detail focused.
- Able to manage crises
- Able to mitigate potential risks
- Good at multitasking
- Knowledgeable of health and safety laws

- Flexible
- Flexible
- And, Flexible

Great 1st ADs are hard to come by, but are worth every penny. Most directors can make really good films without a 1st AD, but they typically can't focus on the subtle nuances of the story, while staying within budget, unless they have a 1st AD.

Directing a Storyboard Artist

There are times when a director needs to pre-visualize a scene. It might be to speed the camera set-up during a shoot, help the FX team choreograph a difficult series of moves, or help an investor better understand the visual elements of a story they are backing. In every case, there are seven key elements a director can use to help a storyboard artist.

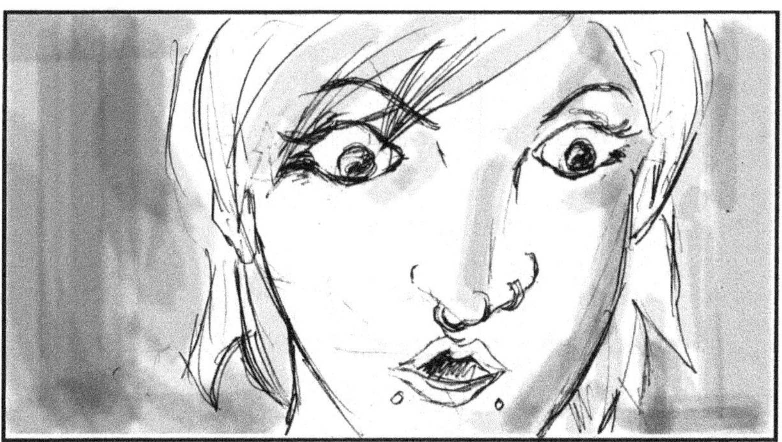

Legend of the Lightstone was the first picture I worked on that required storyboards for the FX team. It was used to determine gear, equipment and background plates needed to capture my vision. Since ILM was to produce the effects, I had the privilege of working with their staff storyboard artist, who gave me a few pointers.

Here are the key elements that directors can use to help their storyboard artist:

1. Predetermine the Aspect Ratio

Inform the artist what ratio he should use for his frame. A film is shot with various aspect ratios, depending on its initial release format. The following is a list of board formats and its corresponding dimensions (length:height):

- Anamorphic film is 2.35:1
- Standard theatrical format is 1.85:1
- HD Video or 16X9 is 1.78:1
- Super 16mm or European theatrical is 1.66:1
- The old TV standard was 1.33:1

2. Describe The Shot Choice

The shot is made up of a location, set-up or angle, lighting, composition, and lens length. The position of the camera and its distance from the subject can be referred to using common shot types:

- EWS (Extreme Wide Shot)
- WS or LS (Wide Shot or Long Shot)
- FS (Full Shot – Entire person)
- Cowboy Shot (Framed from head to mid thigh)
- MS (Medium Shot – Framed head to hips)
- CU (Close Up Shot – Framed top of head to base of neck)
- Choker Shot (Framed forehead to chin)
- ECU (Extreme Close Up – Framed eyebrows to bottom of lips)

- OTS (Over the Shoulder Shot – Camera looks over shoulder of one character at the other character as a CU or MS)
- POV (Point of View – Follows a CU of the character whose view will be shown and is a MS or WS, but can be a CU of what he's focused on)
- Reverse Shot (Shot 180 degrees in the opposite direction of the previous shot)
- Reaction Shot (Shot of character's emotional response that is typically a CU or MS)
- High Angle (Shot from an angle above the characters)
- Bird's Eye View (Shot from up where birds fly)
- Overhead Shot (Shot from directly above the characters)
- Worm's Eye View (Low angle shot looking up at the characters)

3. Establish Eye Line Based On Emotions

The artist is not able to raise or lower a camera, but he can change the horizon line in his drawing to create a similar effect of changing the camera height. By raising the horizon, the drawing will look like the camera is higher than the character and diminish his power. By lowering the horizon line, the camera appears below the character, making him look more powerful.

In the same way, the artist can draw the character looking into the camera as in a frontal shot, or turned 90 degrees for a profile shot, or create a ¾ shot or ¾ frontal shot. This decision will also impact the emotional flavor of the scene.

4. Specify Camera Movement

Consideration must be given to camera movement. Common types of movements include: pans, tilts, dolly shots, push in/push out or trucking shots, boom, crane, steadicam, or specialized shots like zolly (pushing in while zooming out), sleeper, corkscrew, or dutch tilt. By describing the use of a long or short lens, or zoom allows the artist to blur foreground or background objects to create a depth of field effect. It would also be prudent to mention other specialty lenses like the fisheye lens, if you want the artist to render the frame in a similar fashion as the lens.

5. Create A Blocking Diagram

The artist needs to know how many characters are in the shot and their positions within the frame at any given time. This includes their movement and placement. An over-the-head diagram can be sketched with the camera to help the artist visualize each character's position, relative to the camera and composition. If multiple camera angles are shown in the diagram, it is important to draw in the camera axis line so the artist won't accidentally flip the audience's POV.

6. Pitch The Story

To give a feel for the scene and the director's vision, the story can be shared similar to a pitch. This is accomplished by sharing with the artist what happens physically, visually and emotionally in the scene. The more the artist understands the tone of the scene and its action, the more the artist's style will match the vision.

7. Create A Thumbnail Sketch

My explanations to the artist typically generate storyboards to my liking 80 percent of the time. The remaining 20 percent needs to be reworked or adjusted. If I draw a thumbnail sketch for composition purposes, the artist is able to create a frame that matches my vision.

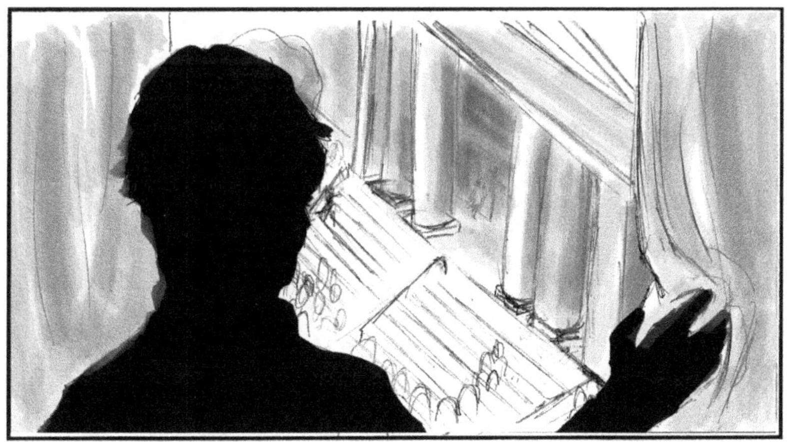

Keep in mind that a stagnant storyboard may need to be altered for animatics. If the artist knows that an animatic will be created for a living reel or business purposes, he may choose to draw his boards in layers for various types of output as required. By using a layered approach, he can also save time, should only portions of a board need to be altered.

Visualizing the Screenplay in Shots

I used to write a monthly column on screenwriting that was published to a subscriber base of about 16,000 writers. The vast majority of the writers were novelists or magazine columnists with an interest in writing screenplays. Some sent me samples of their work, which always amazed me. But I found it ironic that they couldn't write a screenplay of any value.

Here is one example that might read better as a novel, but it died as a screenplay:

> "An ominous and foreboding spirit filled the eyes of those standing over the cold body. The disheveled little boy bent down and nudged the stiff once more. He was sure the man was dead and purposely emptied his pockets in hopes of buying a doughnut at the end of the day."

Screenplays need to be visualized for the camera or the director's eye. Using the word "cold" in reference to the body can't play on film, but "blue" or "deathly gray" can. The same goes for the ominous and foreboding spirit. Unless you are prepared for special effects, those words just eat up precious screenplay space and don't belong. The same holds true for nudging something, "once more", especially if we didn't see the first nudge.

Depending on the screenwriting coach, some may accept words like "purposely" emptied his pockets, while others wouldn't. Some feel it is good to hint to the actor that they need to be purposeful in their actions of removing the coins. Others feel that the actors are capable of determining their own motivation for reaching into the pocket of a dead person.

But both types of teachers would agree that actors can't show the phrase "in hopes of buying a doughnut at the end of the day." Without dialog or a set-up scene, there is no way for the audience to suddenly think, "Oh, good, now he can buy a doughnut."

A reader's script might be written as follows:

The little boy's eyes widen. His feet stand next to a corpse. He glances at his ragged clothes and rubs his belly. One of his friends nods toward the body. The boy bends down and nudges the bluish skin. Nothing moves. He puts his hand into the deceased's pants pocket. His eyes widen as he pulls out a fist of coins. The boys cheer. The little boy steps back, turns and runs. The boys chase after him screaming for the money.

Here is the scene written for a shooting script:

```
CLOSE ON: A little boy's EYES stare at:

A LIFELESS CORPSE

wears a fine suit.

THE BOY

glances at his ragged clothes. His hand moves
over his belly.

ON EYES

as they close.

A GROUP OF BOYS
```

watch him closely.

THE LITTLE BOY'S EYES

slowly open.

HIS FRIEND

nods toward the body.

THE LITTLE BOY

bends down and nudges the bluish skin. Nothing moves.

ANGLE ON PANTS POCKET

He runs his hand into the deceased's pants pocket.

ON EYES

as he pulls his hand out.

ON FIST

as his hand opens revealing coins.

A GROUP OF BOYS

cheer!

ANGLE ON LITTLE BOY'S FEET

stepping backwards.

ON THE LITTLE BOY

as he turns and runs.

A GROUP OF BOYS

```
chase after him screaming for the money.
```

All three are the same story with varying levels of visualization. It is critical for the screenwriter to paint a picture according to the type of script he is writing. However, the more visual language used to describe the action, the easier it is to translate the story from paper to screen.

The 180° Rule

There are four to five different names for the 180° Rule, depending on when it was taught. The rule was first acknowledged in the early 1920s. The film attributed with its origin is the 1925 film *The Battleship Potemkin.*

The below diagram illustrates the rule. The dotted line is an imaginary line that represents the action line or the camera line. The camera is allowed to be set up anywhere on one side of the line, giving it 180° of understandable angles that can be shot. The gray camera broke the rule by crossing the line, which will create an image that may not be readily understood and can confuse the audience.

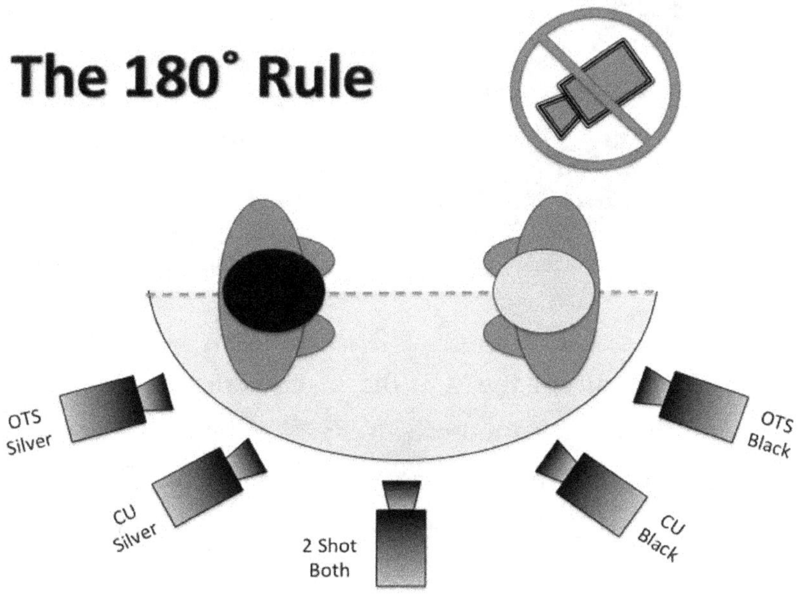

By viewing the shots, each camera position capture will help bring visual clarity to the rule. The below picture is the establishing shot captured by the "2 Shot Both" camera. The image helps the audience to understand that the officer with black hair is screen left, looking right.

The audience also understands that when the black haired officer is looking screen right, he is looking at the silver haired officer. And, if he is looking screen left, he is looking away from the silver haired officer.

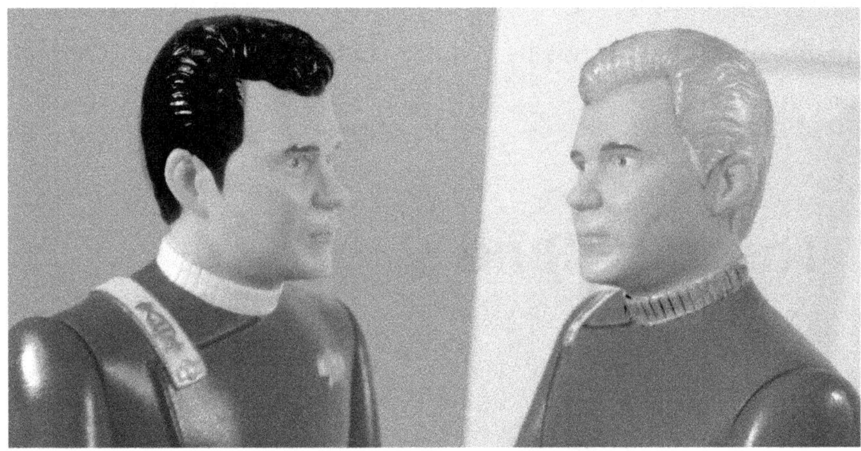

The next picture is the "CU Black" camera that captures the close-up of the black-haired officer. Because he is looking screen right, the audience knows he's still looking at the silver-haired officer, even though he is not on screen. It is a simple illusion that our minds fill in to create continuity of story and understanding.

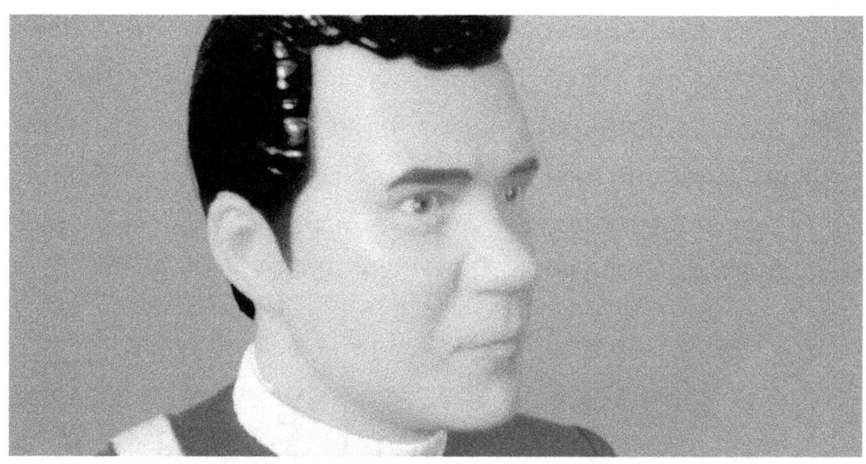

The next picture is the "CU Silver" camera that captures the close-up of the silver haired officer. Because he is looking screen left, the audience knows he's still looking at the black haired officer even though he is not on screen. By cutting back and forth between the two close-ups, the audience has the illusion that they are talking face to face.

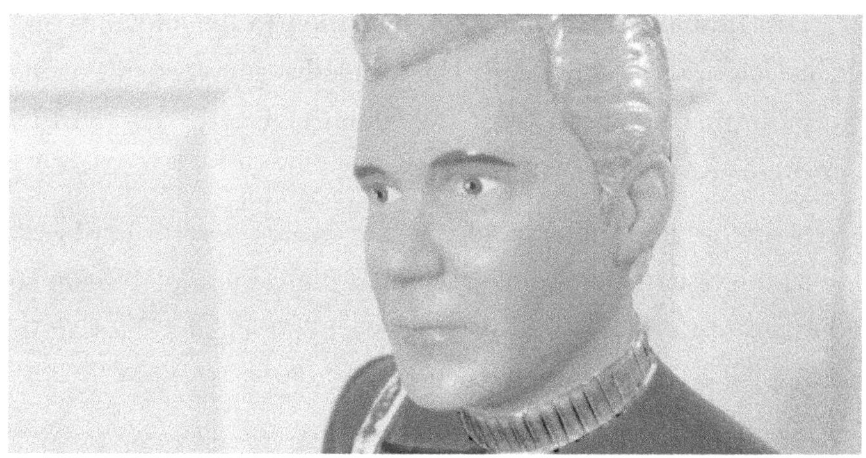

The next picture is the "Gray" camera that captures a close-up of the purple officer from across the action line. While the black-haired officer is still looking at the silver-haired officer, the audience thinks he turned around and is looking away from the silver-haired officer because of the direction he is facing, which is not the same as the establishing two shot.

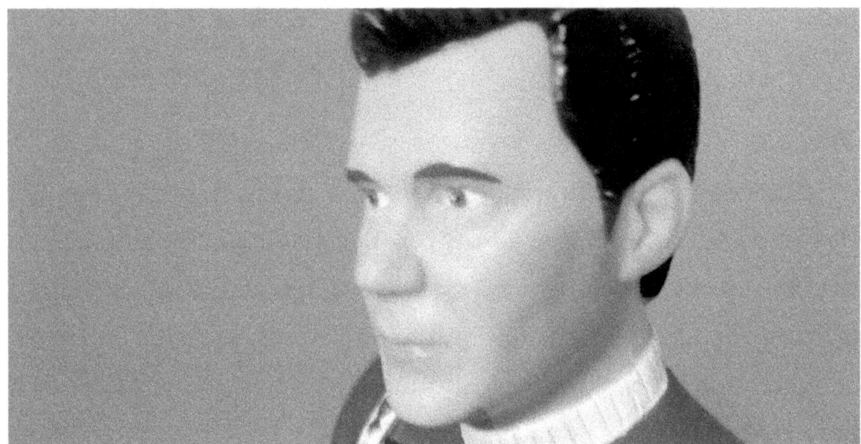

This flipping of the image is unsettling to the audience and creates significant confusion. This pulls the audience out of the story until they can reorient themselves to the virtual surroundings they are witnessing.

Now that you understand the rule and why you can't break the action line, there is a way to cheat the camera placement so you can move all away around the full 360° circle. This can be accomplished by rotating the action line.

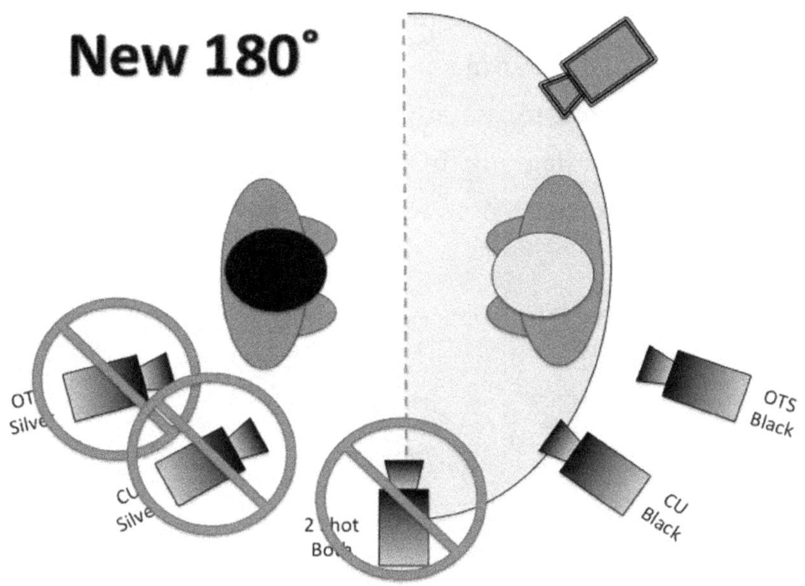

Rotating the axis is a difficult skill that requires a few extra rules for understanding.

First, whenever you change shots, the next camera has to be placed at a minimum angle of 30° difference to the previous angle. If this is not done, then the shot will appear to be a jump cut, which can be disorienting to the audience.

The second rule is that you can't move from the "CU Silver" camera to the "Gray" camera because it would be visually jolting for the audience. You can, however, make the movements incremental between 30° and 90° at a time. This means that you can move from the "CU Black" camera to the "Gray" camera, without jolting the audience. But once you've arrived at the "Gray" camera, you can't go back to the "CU Silver" without moving back incrementally as you rotate the axis back.

In other words, once you've moved from the "CU Black" camera to the "Gray" camera, the action line is now perpendicular to its starting point. This gives you a new 180° rule that allows you to use any of the camera setups from the right side of the diagram, instead of the cameras across the bottom of the diagram.

Cinematographers Drop the Golden Rule

Since Kodak released the first consumer camera, they have promoted the use of the Golden Rule of Thirds to improve amateur photography, thereby selling more film. Millions of novices took to the streets with their newest compact cameras and shot to their hearts content, only to realize that they either had no taste in composition or that there was still a huge difference between their attempts compared to that of professionals.

What most would-be photographers didn't realize was that professionals didn't use the Golden Rule, but instead used the Golden Mean or the Golden Ratio. The main reason for this difference was due to the complexity involved that amateurs had no passion to learn. The professionals, on the other hand, were now competing with a slew of amateurs and needed to distinguish their work through excellent composition.

Kodak promoted the Golden Rule because it was fast and easy to learn, especially on a camera using a 4:3 format ratio. The Photographer looks through the viewfinder, imagines that it's divided equally into 9 boxes (3 across and 3 down) and aligns the picture so the most important element is at one of the intersections.

The Golden Mean is more difficult to understand and allows the photographer to use it with any format ratio. It is not only mathematical, but also very present in nature, such as in the natural spire of a seashell, the rectangular layering of triangles perpendicular to each angle or the rotated rectangles inside rectangles.

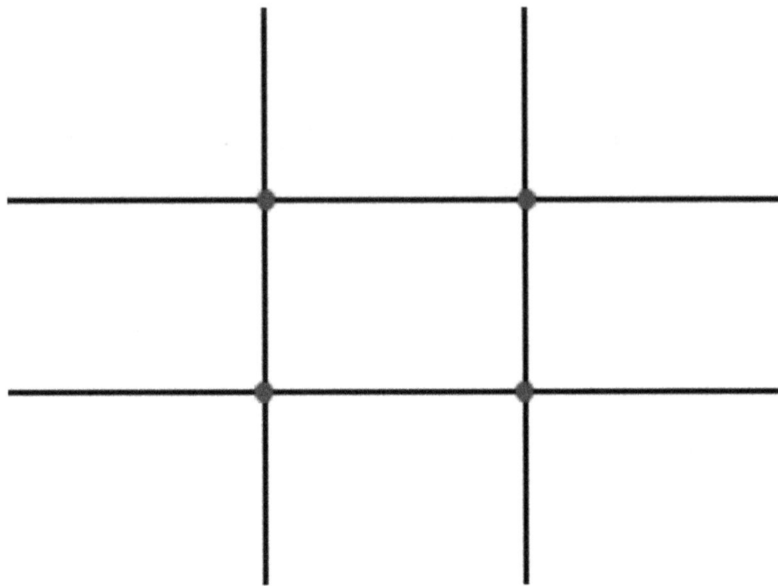

Golden Rule of Thirds

This divine composition mathematically works out to a 1:1. 618... ratio.

Here is the formula...

$$\varphi = \frac{1+\sqrt{5}}{2} = 1.6180339887\ldots$$

Cinematographers choose the Golden Mean over the Rule of Thirds, but seldom have time during a shoot to address the math in order to frame and capture the perfect composition. Instead, they get a feel for what looks good by practicing the proper framing so often that their eye goes right to the Golden Mean points without calculation.

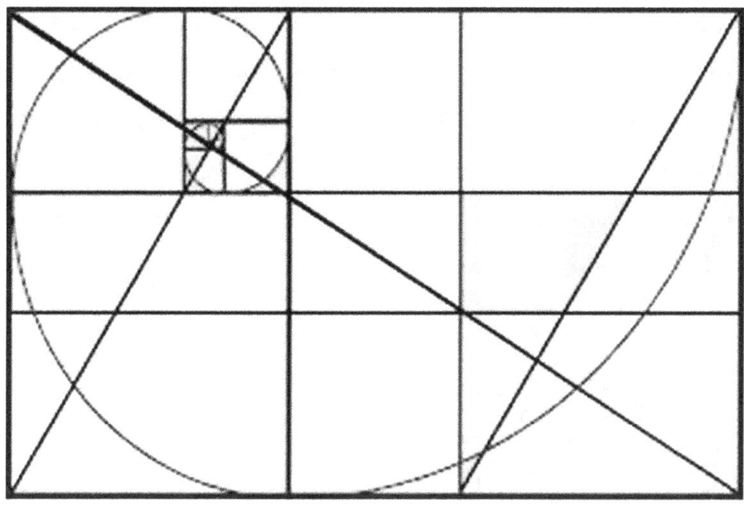

Golden Mean

I was first taught the Golden Mean when I was shooting a documentary for CBS back in my early 20s. I struggled with the math until a more experienced pro took me under his wing and shared his secret to capturing the right composition on the fly. His trick was so easy and effective that I won several awards for composition. I was also able to use the technique for still work and won prestigious composition awards from Kodak and Polaroid.

Instead of attempting the math, the pro told me to divide the screen by 5 units followed by 8 units, or 8 units followed by 5 units, both vertically and horizontally. This meant that the entire frame had 13 vertical units and 13 horizontal units. The place where the two ratios intersected was the golden composition point. This allowed me to memorize the placement of the composition points based on the size and shape of the frame.

If I was shooting at 1:2.35, I could find the composition point just as fast as I did shooting at 1:1.85 or any other frame size.

With this new form of composition, the sizing of the frame did not matter, nor did the perf pull down system. It no longer mattered if the frame was single perf, 4 perf or even 8 perf. This also meant it transitioned quickly to HD, regardless of the sizes or dimensions of the digital censors or the 16X9 relative fields from RED, SONY, ARRI, etc..

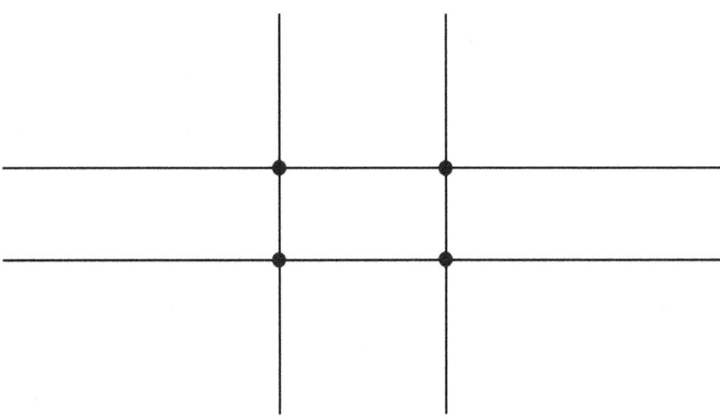

Golden Mean

The Director of Photography is always concerned about the format, lenses, lights and composition. Each element helps capture the director's vision onto the media of choice. And, because movies are pictures in motion, the other factor that concerns DPs is the camera movement.

The good news is that the Golden Mean can quickly be reset during dolly, crane, or steadicam shots. A well-practiced camera movement that ties in with the actor's blocking might have a series of focus changes and shifts in composition. Using the Golden Mean allows for the constant changing of the composition on the fly and looks great on screen.

Dynamic Composition

I was thinking about my dad over the weekend and recalled several lessons he taught me in filmmaking. One was about dynamic composition with a moving camera. Composition is something taught heavily to still photographers, but is rarely taught to cinematographers.

Dynamic film composition is a tool used by the director of photography to support the director's visual choices for telling his story. Simply put, it's the composing and recomposing of a shot while the camera or actors are moving. The camera needs to encompass the same visual rhythm the director implements with the actors, and the duration of each shot must take into consideration the effect perception has on the audience.

The cinematographer starts with the understanding that his composition will create an immediate, instinctual response in the eye of the audience. He must also comprehend that each viewer will have a different ability to understand the composition, thereby affecting the way each person emotes in accordance with the story.

Strong composition within a still picture can quickly help a cinematographer understand the audience's eye movement, just like shooting from a locked down camera. However, movement in this decade is king, and every shot requires a variety of camera adjustments to capture a frame that stirs the emotions.

The following elements impact the effectiveness of dynamic composition:

- A subject moving in or out of frame

- The anticipation of a subject moving in or out of frame
- A shift in focus from a background to a foreground subject and visa versa
- A change in texture from hard to soft focus
- Strong movement of a subject within a static frame
- The variation of close-up and long shots
- The camera following a subject
- The synchronization of the actors to the camera movement
- The blocking of the actors to isolate a character within the right focal plane
- The movement of the camera on a dolly, crane, or jib
- The camera's angle to sightlines

I know I'm missing several examples, but I believe the importance of blocking the shots for significance is understood, especially when the camera is in motion. The more movements the camera or actors execute, the more adjustments are required on focus, framing, and set up.

The duration of a shot and the expectation of the audience also play a significant role in dynamic composition. The longer the duration, the easier it is for the audience to discern the elements of a shot and make certain mental or emotional judgments. The faster the shot, the more instinctual or intuitive the scene has to play out in order to keep the audience focused on the story.

The director works with the cinematographer much the same way a conductor works with a musician. He desires to capture the right mood, feel and emotion in a shot, just as a conductor generates the same from the score. Both seek to bring a unique experience to the audience and a variety of rhythm. The director takes the audience on an emotional journey that heightens at the climax and soon resolves into having had a great motion picture experience.

Visual rhythm seems to be an overlooked art today, while still being an important aspect of a movie. Some films easily studied to better understand dynamic composition include:

- The Battleship Potemkin
- Ivan the Terrible
- Stagecoach
- The French Connection

While other films can be studied, the above films were built around the impact of its visual rhythm. Some directors take this visual technique beyond the camera and work closely with production designers and costume designers to help them heighten the impact of a story's emotional pulse. The director owns the depth to which the team will work on the visual rhythm of the story, but the cinematographer is responsible for his team capturing it.

Shaky Camera Technique

Audiences have complained for years about some camera shaking to be a distraction rather than artistic. They can tell when the device fails and pulls the audience out of the story. This makes the viewer cognizant of sitting in a theater or staring at an HD screen that accentuates the movement. The artistic value has been questioned for years, due to the equal number of successes the technique achieved.

I believe the key to the shaky camera technique's success is directly related to the emotions of the storyline. It typically won't be effective if a first-time filmmaker wants to use the technique because it's cool, rather than knowing if it fits the story. Even the experts struggle with when to use the device, but those who have mastered it are the ones that understand how to build emotions with an image.

My dad shot film before I was ever born and by my junior high years he suggested how I could improve my filmmaking. He told me the simplest thing: Motion pictures are all about motion. He further explained that if the actors aren't moving, the camera should be.

If we take this simple lesson to its obvious conclusion, we must determine what will be happening in the shot and to what degree or level the added movement must be at. In stage shows, the actor moving toward the audience is comparable to a close up, just as the actor moving up stage is similar to a long shot. Each relative position sets a different parameter of emotional values.

When an actor gently whispers in a close up, the audience feels drawn into a new level of intimacy. And, obviously stated, the actor shouting across the room demands a wider shot to capture the space needed for the appropriate volume.

Camera movement is similar. If the handheld is shooting an intimate scene, having the camera bouncing more vigorously makes no sense. Likewise, if the scene is fast paced with lots of movement, keeping the camera moving at the same tempo increases the emotional pull on the audience.

Picture a man and a woman sharing an intimate conversation. The camera is in close and the words are just above a whisper. Having the camera off of the tripod but barely moving gives the audience a sense of freedom and love.

Suddenly the man wakes up from his dream. He jolts to look around the room with the camera following the same intense pattern. Then he sees him – the antagonist with exposed bombs strapped to his chest. The wacko raises the detonator button and laughs. The camera jerks around from the laughter, to the bombs, to the detonator, to our hero, who scrambles down the hallway to get away from the lunatic.

The key is to fit the handheld movement to the emotional level, in conjunction with the pacing of the scene. What makes it difficult is the fine line of error that pulls the audience out of the story if it isn't executed properly.

For instance, what if the camera suggests intimacy, but the actor fails to draw the audience into the intimate moment? Or, in a chase scene the actor isn't running at full speed and the audience can tell, but the camera is frantically moving to preserve some form of tension? It will look silly.

The test to the handheld's movement success is directly correlated to the audience being pulled deeper into story or noticing the camera movement and losing track of the story in any specific moment.

I've seen shows where the camera movement is so well articulated around the emotions of the scene that I found myself physically leaning, subconsciously trying to shift the camera's perspective without being pulled out of the story. I was shifting with the camera, as if I could somehow help the hero make his way through the perplexing situation unharmed. I've also seen films where the camera movements made me feel sick and I willingly turned from the film.

It takes great communication between the director, cinematographer and actor to pull off the shaky camera effect and when done properly it saves time, budget and builds great emotions into a scene.

Getting a Film Produced and Released

Passion Drives the Niche Market

I've spoken to hundreds of filmmakers over the years and one thing still holds true: the stronger their passion, the better their films turn out. This isn't to say the more universally-accepted their films becomes In fact, some passionate films, while making a strong point or accomplishing the filmmakers' mission, are not received well by the public.

The passion is what sparks the creativity and drives the filmmaker to improve his craft. Without it, he makes only films that are overt, obvious or expected. This same difference used to be seen between television and movie houses. TV was cranked out so fast, the plotlines were simple and the messages weak, while motion pictures took advantage of longer production schedules and higher attention to details leading to message.

Today films are based on remakes and television episodes are constantly re-run. Passion seems to be at an all time low.

I made a Christmas e-card last year, based on a specific passion that was stirring within me. I received word back from several people who had very different perspectives on what I created. One person voiced her disappointment, while another was excited that it caused her Millennial to ask questions about how the message was related to Christmas – the exact response I had hoped for.

Passionate filmmakers that have numerous untold stories that must get out into the public find it hard to receive a plethora of public response. Some filmmakers can't handle the pressures from those that disliked their work and others change their work to meet up with the praises of the people. Both types of responses dull the passion and reduce the number of films released.

The passionate filmmaker that continues to move forward listening to his heart, is the one whose films are emotionally gripping for the specific audience for which they were made. An example would be the film *Courageous*. The Kendrick Brothers know their audience well and found their film to be a huge hit within that niche. However, people outside of their audience didn't understand their fans' passion for the story.

The Twilight Series had the same affect. Millions of people went to see the films and raved about them. But those outside of the niche market couldn't understand what the buzz was about.

There seems to be only two possibilities for the filmmaker: finding the right audience to share his passion; or, altering the story to fit a larger audience, which might risk the level of passion that makes its way to the screen. Without passion, few in the audience care about the story.

It's the passion within the filmmaker that must deliver the message, for without it, the film lacks value. Said more simply, a passionate filmmaker can present a message that changes people's perspectives and hearts.

Unfortunately, the opposite is also true. Watching a film from a less passionate filmmaker isn't worth the admission price.

Creating Buzz for Film

I've witnessed filmmakers fail publicly without knowing it. Several have attempted to raise funds without first establishing PR guidelines, and others have attempted to release their films without priming the PR pump. The one thing these filmmakers had in common is that they were disappointed in their final results, and had no idea why they failed.

In this new age of Internet, there are seven steps that have become essential in protecting a filmmaker from PR failure. The mathematics on these steps is straightforward and filmmakers that adhere to them will see their visibility rise.

Here are the seven steps needed to succeed:

1. Start with Niche Market

I recently coached a filmmaker to get verbal commitments from donors in advance of raising his funds on the software program Kickstarter in hopes of sparking interest from others on the first day of the campaign. He emailed his friends and family, but didn't ask for any commitments. As a result, he raised zero funds.

Everyone wants national exposure and the best way to get that exposure starts with communicating locally, then regionally, nationally, and finally globally. Independent films use this same standard by releasing in a specific region, gaining press and buzz, then moving to more screens nationally. These same standards are used to increase PR.

If the product can't be established "locally", it can be established in an affinity community or niche market. Once the buzz rises, moving it to the regional equivalent is easier, due to the existing groundswell of PR in the niche market. It takes only one re-Tweet from the right person to get the message to millions.

2. Timing is Everything

I was excited by a buzz that increased last summer over a drama I wanted to see. By Thanksgiving I gave up on the movie, as it still hadn't released. Ten months passed and it still isn't out, yet I continually see sporadic promotions about it coming soon. Frankly, I'm so tired of hearing about this film that there is no way it can ever live up to its long hype cycle. The filmmakers will be lucky to get a real audience or even attract distribution at this point.

To achieve that one re-Tweet that puts a message into the hands of millions of people at just the right time, the campaign needs to start three to six months ahead of schedule creating the buzz and groundswell. Perfectly timed messages can give a product an increase in sales by ten or twenty times. However, a poorly-timed message can undermine everything done to date.

I recall a conversation with Ken Taylor of Tyndale House Publishers. He said sales of his paraphrased Bible amounted to a couple copies a day, which his son Mark packed and shipped, using supplies he kept under his bed. After Amy Grant mentioned how great the Living Bible was at one of her concerts, the daily volume jumped into the thousands and the family moved distribution into a large warehouse. Amy's simple comment drove Mark Taylor to become the president of one of the largest independent publishers in America. I can only imagine what a single Tweet might do from the right person.

3. Plan and Schedule

One rock star shared with me the seven to eight "off the cuff" publicity stunts of which he was a part that generated significant press for his band and other co-promoted artists. He gave several examples that MTV, the king of impromptu press, took months to prepare.

It takes a lot of work to prepare specific messages to key audiences and have it come off in an impromptu manner. To accomplish the sizeable buzz that impromptu events create, everything must be reduced to writing and scheduled six to twelve months in advance.

Many filmmakers try to handle all the press themselves, but for publicity to work properly, the PR person has to develop professional relationships with all the press sources that reach the artist's niche and expansion markets. The press needs far more information to publish than they have available, which allows the relationship to help both parties involved.

4. Differentiate the Artist/Product

A filmmaker complained to me that his product tanked and he didn't understand why. I asked him what he had done to brand his product and he said that it wasn't necessary because it was just like…, then he named a product I had already seen.

So, I asked, "Since I already saw the original product, why would I want to see your version?" He had no answer, which explains why no one wanted to see it.

Media sources do not promote "also" films. They don't have to because they can promote the "real one". The only way around this situation is to differentiate your film and promote its uniqueness. The press and the audience need to know what makes your film different. They need to understand why they have to see it.

The majority of all independent films is some form of a knockoff, which gains little audience. The few films that take off typically have something so unique about it that people are drawn to it. That uniqueness must come out in the press for enough coverage to draw a large audience. Without it, the film will fail.

5. Be On Message

I watched three clips of a filmmaker interviewed on TV about his latest release. Since I had previewed the film, I knew exact what three points would drive the audience to see his film or buy it on video. I was amazed that he didn't mention one of those three points. During one segment, the host started out excited about the film and quickly lost his energy when the filmmaker rambled about meaningless things. The interviewer had nowhere to go and the audience was convinced not to see the film.

Every film has a message that needs to get out, and every audience needs to hear about the message in a particular way for them to spend money on the film. Developing the message is critical and making sure everyone interviewed is on the same message is important.

Putting together a guideline of key phrases and context or communication will strengthen the overall message and point the audience in the same direction, regardless of the PR opportunity. Deviating from the message will create indiscernible noise and will reduce box office and video sales.

6. Tweet and Retweet

Last week a PR expert that handles several big names told me that her number one tool to generate press is Twitter. She pointed out how all of her press sources follow her and her artists. Each Tweet she sends lands on ten million cell phones within two minutes through Twitter. The last three concerts she promoted sold out within ten minutes after she Tweeted her announcement. They didn't advertise any of those concerts and as a result, saved $25 million in advertising.

Most filmmakers are on Twitter, but don't know how to use the tool. Having a PR person on staff helps develop the message and increase the number of followers. Some filmmakers have just started to follow as many people as they could find that are interested in the genre they produce. However, recent studies show that following more people than follow you will not increase your readership.

Tweeting is all about finding the people interested in your product. Following people that might be interested is very different than finding those that are interested. Once you have

500 thousand people true fans, you'll be able to generate serious sales every time you Tweet your latest product.

7. Learn from Madonna

I watched an interview with one of the top People magazine reporters. He was talking about how he gets story ideas from Twitter and why he avoids certain stories and takes others. When he summarized his suggestions for getting more press, he said that anyone who wants to get serious about PR should pay attention to Madonna, the queen of PR.

Controversy is one of Madonna's tools, but it isn't the most important one. Any time she releases information about a new concert, video or book, she first stimulates the market with things that prompt discussion – She gets everyone talking about her regardless of it being good or bad.

The key to her promotion is making sure that the buzz is always directly related to her product. It is never related to a cause or political view. In fact, the only other artist that perfectly followed suit was Michael Jackson. Both artists generated more buzz and free press than any others in entertainment history.

Cross promotions follow the same key steps above, but require collaboration and lots of planning. Because ancillary products might be involved, it is critical that only the main product is promoted. Once in the store, the audience will find the other products in the display – whether in a physical store or an online store.

Trailer Elements that Generate Buzz

I watched a trailer for a new independent film that seemed to be a mini- story in its own right. The clips were so well put together and the ending so clear that I was completely satisfied and didn't need to see the film. That same day I saw another trailer that gave me just enough information to be curious, which drove my need to see more. Curiosity festered within me until I had to see the film.

Trailers must create that sense of desire and curiosity to draw an audience. By raising a question in the audience's mind, the filmmaker forces the audience to seek out the answer and purchase a ticket. Unfortunately, filmmakers struggle with knowing what part of the film should be promoted and what part withheld for the film's theatrical release.

This delicate balance can be achieved using a few rules:

Use Set Pieces From Act 1 & 2A

Set pieces are scenes that are designed to have an obvious imposing effect on the audience. They are ideal for trailers. They are also the scenes that stand out, messaging the film is unique and special. When done correctly, the scenes generate a good deal of marketing buzz.

A strong set piece withstands the test of time. Many remember the *Star Wars* light saber battle between Darth and Obi-wan Kenobi. Another iconic set piece was the scene in which Indiana Jones runs away from the giant boulder. And who could ever forget the DeLorean racing across the wet mall parking lot to vanish into a pair of fire trails in *Back to the Future*?

Set pieces distinguish a film and drive the buzz that skyrockets that title to success. It becomes the story's leverage enticing audiences to shell out money for tickets. It also conveys to the press that the film is new and fresh, making it newsworthy and promotable.

Use Hero's Flaw and Set Up

The hero has to be likeable or his situation relatable to the audience. By introducing him in a humorous way, or by establishing some form of crisis that people can relate to, helps build a desire in the audience to find out how the hero will deal with his dilemma.

Establishing the hero's flaw or problem is also prudent, but use only enough of it to establish the question of how the problem will be resolved. "Why" answers satisfy and "what" answers generate conversation, leading to ticket sales.

Never Use Anything From Act 3

By Act 3, the audience knows exactly where the story is headed, but doesn't know how the climax will arrive. If something is used from Act 3 for publicity, the audience will easily determine the film's outcome before they see the movie. Act 3 elements are sacred and are considered off limits in the promotion of a film. However, some companies have used Act 3 scenes in a misleading way to entice the audience, but unless you want the audience to feel ripped off, I don't recommend that strategy.

Don't Use The Theme

The theme is typically associated with some form of moral or social lesson. It's a part of the story that should never be revealed during promotions, because once a person understands the lesson there is no need to see the film. Many times the lesson might seem forced, unless it's properly woven into the full story, which a trailer cannot do.

Raise The Universal Question

Every film raises a question in the audience's mind that needs to be fulfilled or completed. The trailer also needs to raise the question, but in a way that causes the audience to wonder how the hero is going to accomplish it. This drives the audience's desire to see the film and find out how the hero succeeds.

The above rules will keep the filmmaker safe from giving out important information that needs to be saved for the film. They also position the filmmaker's mindset to focus on the action he wants the audience member to take, which is purchasing a ticket to watch the film and get the answer to the questions haunting his or her mind.

Managing the Press

Motion picture releases force actors, directors and writers to deal with the press more often than most business or government figures. Yet those in filmmaking get taught about how to manage the press far less often than those in the political or Fortune 100 arenas.

There are several important points to cover in managing the all-important press:

Don't Try To Control The Press

The media is made up of professionals and attention-getting bloggers that use people skills to get human stories. No one likes to be controlled and the press is no different. It's a people business that is all about promoting various levels of celebrities. The key to managing the press is to understand who is reputable and what audience they serve. Without this basic knowledge, you will send a message that has a high chance of being misquoted to the wrong people.

Build Long Term Relationships

Developing relationships with the right reporter, who attracts the right audience, empowers you to get a clean message to the right people. This ideal takes time to nurture, as both the filmmaker and the reporter must work to develop trust in each other.

Package The Story For The Right Reporter

Journalists and reporters are always interested in the right story, but much of their time is spent sorting through a myriad of stories that don't fit their audience. For instance, a church sending Easter service information to a sports writer is a waste of everyone's time. All too often press releases don't get to the right editors or journalists because those trying to get exposure didn't take time to research their ideal audiences and write what type of information they read.

Don't Grab Free Press, Provide Free News

Every newspaper and radio station knows you want free press to promote your film, but no one wants to help you, unless they benefit from it. By providing the right reporter with the right content for the right audience, your story becomes newsworthy. This makes the press look good, while you're introducing your film to a new audience. When that happens, everyone wins.

Know What's On And Off The Record

Everything is on the record unless agreed to otherwise, and the tape recorder is turned off and the pencil set down. Giving background information isn't typically quoted, but helps the reporter gain an understanding of the circumstances in order to build their story properly. With this all said, it's important to understand that a person being interviewed must be careful in their responses to make sure the reporter doesn't take anything out of context.

By managing the press with the above key points, word about your film will get out to your primary audience, who will be inspired to support it with strong ticket sales. They might even re-Tweet your promotional information to help their friends.

Three Secrets to Box Office Success

There are a few steps that faith and family filmmakers need to compete against today's secular tastes that drive PG-13 and R-rated films. These steps seem to go against the norms of the G and PG rated film, but they do not hurt the films. However, each filmmaker has to consider to what depth he or she takes these recommendations.

1. Develop Strong Conflict

I use the GAC^2 (Gack Squared) principle in all but transition scenes. The letters stand for Goal, Action, Consequence and Conflict. Every scene must have Mick (**M**ost **I**mportant **C**haracter **K**now) experience GAC^2 in numerous scenes or the audience gets bored.

In the beginning of the scene the story has to reveal Mick's goal, just like in the beginning of the movie, the story has to reveal Mick's overarching or universal goal. But within each scene Mick has a minor goal that needs to be obtained, like trying to get to someone for information, convince them to change their mind or influence a person to hand over an answer's whereabouts.

When the goal is well established, the audience has something to cheer for and can be taken on an emotional ride, especially once the action is taken. The action could be crossing the room, throwing a drink in someone's face, or letting go of an embraced loved one.

Since the scene most likely has a supporting character to help reveal more about Mick, he or she has to respond in a way that reveals conflict. If Mick crosses the room toward a pretty blonde holding the answers to his forgotten life, a bodyguard might create conflict by stepping between him and her. Or, maybe Mick throws a drink in the boyfriend's face to lose him in order to talk to the blonde, but instead he pulls a knife on Mick. Or, maybe Mick is dancing at a wedding reception with a loved one when he spots the blonde, he releases the loved one and walks toward the blonde, causing the loved one to jealously shout that she wants a divorce.

You can see that the possibilities bring interest to the scene. It also drives a question that forces the audience to desire seeing the next scene in order to find out how the story unfolds.

2. Give The Audience New Ideas To Consider

This is the hardest thing for most faith and family filmmakers, because it requires pushing their audience out of their comfort zone, which conservative families do not like. It can create animosity and shut down the filmmaker's future.

Without it, the audience goes home saying, "Gee, that film was swell, but it's just like all the others." If the story doesn't reveal something interesting, unique or life changing, then it should be a minor video release and not a silver screen presentation. Most people aren't willing to pay $10 a head for a film that confirms they are living right or are better off than others.

People only find value in revelation and growth, yet those two items are the two things that no one wants to experience because it takes change and energy. Most people don't want to think through a film, yet they talk about how stupid the show is unless it caused them to think.

People hate change, especially if the change is how they think. However, if the filmmaker has the audacity to attempt to change the minds of the audience, he will receive significant controversy and, consequentially, box office success. That is something few faith and family filmmakers are willing to bring to the table. They would prefer to make less money and not risk their mediocre careers.

3. Give The Audience Something Never Seen

In the time of franchises regurgitating copycat films, the audience is hungry for something they've never seen before. I mean, how many different takes on Spiderman can we see without saying, "Enough already!"

Forest Gump, Amadeus and Rain Man won Oscars for Best Picture and were huge successes because the audience was introduced to a new character worthy of mental and emotional exploration. Similarly, locations that prompted eye-opening visual fascination and Oscars or box office successes include Avatar, Dances with Wolves and Slumdog Millionaire. Several films that combined both elements won an Oscar, like Shindler's List, Gone with the Wind and Braveheart.

Most of these films took more production days and larger budgets to accomplish, something that is rare among faith and family films. That's not to say it can't be done, as Slumdog Millionaire was a low budget film that introduced audiences to new locations, cultures and characters.

Competing for screen time and drawing in the audience in this day and age demands the above three points be a part of every story. The question is, which faith and family filmmaker will risk his career to make a film that gives the audience a huge payoff mentally and emotionally, and drives interest in an Oscar nomination?

Tips for a Filmmaker of Short Films

My experience judging film festivals leads me to believe that the number one issue creating a chasm between a great film and a lousy one is the story structure or lack of it. While experience and technical expertise plays a role in making a great film, most filmmakers could have jumped ahead of the competition by improving their story structure.

Story structure for a short film is as simple as having a beginning, middle and an end. Some filmmakers expand the formula by adding on an epilogue. However, this simple three-act structure is the one thing that drives the story forward and creates a desire in viewers to see the story to completion. Without it, the audience asks why they wasted their time.

The following tips can help a filmmaker establish a story structure:

Create A Likeable Character

A short film doesn't have the ability to develop a unique or paradoxical character, so simplify things by making him or her likeable. In the first scene, show the character doing something that warms the heart of the audience.

Set-Up Your Story In The First Scene

The opening of a short sets the tone, flavor and pace for the entire film. It is important that you make a comedy's opening funny, or a drama's opening tense or an adventure film's opening exciting.

Give Your Character A Challenge To Overcome

It is important that your character has a flaw he has to learn how to overcome during the middle of the show. This prepares him for the big climax wherein he causes the audience to cheer for his victory.

Create A Huge Obstacle

Whether the main character has to overcome nature, an obstacle, or antagonist, he needs to be bigger than life. This will make the character's win even more powerful for the audience.

Give The Audience Time To Reflect

Once the main character succeeds, the audience needs time to emotionally come down from the excitement and realize what happened. Allow the final scene to play a little longer or add in an epilogue.

These simple steps give direction to a short film that most lack. It will cause the viewer to desire a second or third viewing. Without it, the audience will walk away disappointed.

For those filmmakers in a rush due to deadlines or weekend film competitions, they can simply build a short story around the following questions:

- What fun or cool thing can my main character do?
- How can this play out visually and set the tone for my film?
- What is his or her flaw that needs to be overcome?
- What things would block that growth?

- What might happen that allows the main character to use his newfound strengths to overcome what he or she would normally have failed at?
- What is the best way for my main character to celebrate the victory?

The answer to each question creates an outline that will match up with the story structure explained above. By simply following this process, the filmmaker can get into the top 20 percent of competing films. And, with a flair for artistic expression and a clear understanding of technology, the filmmaker can get himself into the winner's circle.

Short Films Require Set-Up

Feature films use the three-act structure originally conceptualized by Shakespeare. It was an obvious structure, since all stories have a beginning, middle and end. The motion picture industry broke it out further due to the size of shooting and editing reels. Films quickly were divided into Act 1, Act 2A, Act 2B and Act 3.

This was further broken down into two action sequences per act. Each action sequence was 12-15 minutes in length, which would fit on a 15-minute reel. In order to fit in commercial TV breaks at the appropriate time, MOWs (Movie of the Week) used eight acts, with each one running 8-12 minutes.

Since these action sequences all have a beginning, middle and end, and clearly tell a portion of the overall story, I decided to see if I could pull a sequence from a feature and use it as a standalone short film. The idea was simple, if you could make eight shorts and later cut them together as a feature, you could release a feature film every few years on a short film budget. But, it didn't work.

Most story sequences work within a feature because the entire concept was developed in Act 1. The needed backstory that led to the sequence was already in the audience's mind after the first half hour of the film, allowing the director to take short cuts in the telling of the story.

It's therefore paramount that all short films are complete stories within themselves, including the following set-up elements:

- Attention getting device to pull audience into the story
- A shared crisis or humorous moment to bond the hero to the audience
- A subtle moment where the hero does something to protect his heart or an inner pain from the past
- An element of risk or unfair treatment as the hero pursues his goal
- A moment that clarifies that the hero is not content with his circumstances
- An inciting incident that starts the story moving
- The hero's call to adventure and his hesitation to respond
- The revelation that a trap is set or negative circumstances will soon come against the hero

The bad news is that writing a great beginning for a quality short film may take just as long as writing one for a feature film, because all films, regardless of length, require the same set-up beats to be effective for the audience. Unfortunately, many filmmakers will take shortcuts in writing their short film by using stereotypes so they don't have to develop their characters.

While characters are more developed in a feature, most sequences do not have self-contained set-up beats and therefore can't be used as standalone shorts. And, without the proper set-up, the audience will perceive the film differently than intended, making it a flop.

Make a Short vs. Find an Angel

Is the key to filmmaking success a short film that goes viral, or an angel that can fund a moneymaking project?

Over the past five years I've chatted with 2000 plus beginning filmmakers confident that if they create the right short film, it will open up doors of incredible opportunity. I've recently talked with scholars that also think the right short film would launch a career. A few friends have also suggested the same.

The truth is that out of the 4,000 plus filmmakers that followed my writings in various e-zines and the 16,000 writers that read my screenwriting column, none of them had a short film launch their career. In fact, out of the 100,000 plus filmmakers attempting to make their mark over the past five years, only two got a shot in Hollywood based on their short film. One's first project crashed and burned and brought demise to his career. The other's career was launched with budgets he had no idea how to manage.

In the meantime, several dozen filmmakers launched new programs into the peripheral market and found enough success to live off it. They started to build an audience and make enough money for additional projects, while living off of its revenue. In my mind, these are the people who have found success.

Unfortunately, few people are able to enter the market at this lower level without some angel providing a break for them. Each one that I've talked with found someone to believe in them enough to front anywhere from $25-$125,000. These filmmakers also relied heavily on the team approach and pulled together the people needed to make the film.

This is the exact opposite of the trend. Numerous people are suggesting that filmmaking is becoming an individual-based process where one extremely talented person runs the whole show, especially in the area of short films. But the proof still resides with those who team together and create a macro studio to make productions outside of the Hollywood system.

The last time I was at a film convention, I bumped into hundreds of arrogant filmmakers that all had extreme talent in one area and mediocre talent in other areas. I suggested that some of them get together to merge their talents and blow everyone away with an exceptional film that utilizes everyone's expertise. They all looked at me like I was nuts, as they were competitors and would never stoop to such a ghastly thought.

I heard from a few friends that the last convention saw weaker films than the previous year. The quality of production and story had dropped. Few of the "competitors" were able to outdo their previous attempts. Most of them failed, resulting in several of the filmmakers changing their careers – all because they wouldn't lower themselves to partner with other experts.

Those sharing the mentality that individual filmmakers must make it on their own see the drop off as a weeding out process that sifts out the real filmmakers. The odd thing is that most of those that gave up had more talent than those that stuck it out. Its sad to realize that the mediocre are now driving parts of the industry that used to be a collaborative art form for master craftsmen.

Notes from Producer Ralph Winter

Ralph Winter is a force to be reckoned with in the film industry and loves to help the next generation of filmmakers. Ralph is part of the bread and butter filmmakers that make a lifelong career in Hollywood. He has watched many rise and disappear over the years.

The feature *Hocus Pocus* brought Ralph more than a decade of notoriety, but his sci-fi work exceeded everyone's expectations with *Star Trek III, IV, V* and *VI; X-Men, X2, X-Men: The Last Stand,* and *X-Men Origins: Wolverine;* and, *Fantastic Four,* and *Fantastic 4: Rising of the Silver Surfer.* He also produced several Frank Peretti titles and other films.

Ralph uses "old school" techniques to get his job done. He pointed out that when it comes to scheduling, he's faster using Post-it® notes on a wall than PAs or interns using their computer scheduling programs. I actually use the wall myself, but I use blank business cards and painter's tape for longer lasting stickiness. It seems to be much faster than any strip board or scheduling program.

Ralph talked about the latest variation of P&L analysis for films with me. In the past, creating a pro-forma chart with high, medium and low expectations was sufficient. However, today's resources tend to come from more diverse sources that may need a little more hand-holding.

Ralph shared the analysis from his latest venture, which showed a breakdown of revenue and expenses for each release window. It was also notated, not as "H, M, or L," but instead, under the following categories: "Downside, Breakeven, Base, and Breakout." With this new type of analysis, the investors can determine the good and bad of each release window and its impact on the other revenue sources. It also allows for the added benefit line that notates the state tax incentive, based on shooting credits for location work.

The discussion got a little more invigorating when we shifted for a time to the standard break even scenario, which is no longer accurate based on the way many films are now being made. The old method and still the "official" standard method is as follows:

$$\text{Breakeven} = 2.5 * (\text{P\&A} + \text{Production Costs})$$

However, with tax incentives, A-list actors taking more back end funds, and low budget films requiring points for a percentage of the cast and crew, the formula is adjusted for almost every independent production today.

Redemptive Leadership Style

Leadership styles have always amazed me. Some leaders I've admired have executed their style flawlessly and others have miserably failed at the style they've attempted to emulate. Both the excellent and the terrible leaders were permanently etched into my mind. The good news is that I know exactly what not to do and what to strive to achieve.

The leadership style I use is called the redemptive leadership style. It is designed for leaders who need to meet the challenge of drawing a person in from the outer fringes, help them to get well connected, and then draw them further into the core or the heart of the business.

The redemptive leader has four key qualities that help him or her to encourage others to their next level in life and business. None of these elements can be easily taught, but are extremely valuable in leading others.

The four qualities include:

Competence

This is all about a person's skills. While it might take into consideration natural inborn talent, it is focused more on the cumulative effect of the leader's education, life experiences, practical skills that bring opportunity, and intuition. It's all about that inner drive or call in a person's life being matched to a strong desire to learn whatever it takes to get to the next level. However, having just the desire is not enough. It must be proactive and proven out through life's natural struggles and circumstances.

Principles

This is the core element that drives who we are. It is the underlying truth that transcends situations. Regardless of what we face, we find ourselves locked into living, according to our deepest principles. It is the very reason we do what it is that we do, especially when no one is looking.

Character

This is far more than knowing right and wrong. It's about knowing who we actually are – the real you and me. It's about being able to accept our strengths and weaknesses, and then choose to discipline ourselves to live in a positive heart-changed manner. If a self-help book were to be written on this topic, it would include chapters on self-awareness, self-management, and self-development.

Transformation

This is where the rubber meets the road. The leader's life has to display actual change and growth. There is no faking it until you make it. Being able to see actual heart changes in yourself and watching yourself become what you're meant to be is critical to achieving the final elements of this leadership style. It is also the one thing that will allow the leader to directly relate to the people that he or she might influence.

Unfortunately, transforming moments can come only out of pain or insight. Those of us that went through the school of hard knocks, felt the heat of the situation and then changed. A few people were fortunate enough to have an inspired "Ah-ha" moment that led to change. Either way, the leader gains final elements that bring success through this leadership style.

Most of the leaders I know that lead with the redemptive leadership style, gained their abilities after facing great tragedy in their lives. They were good people that had to work through significant pain by gaining the skills that would get them back to some sense of normalcy. During the struggle back, their mettle was tested. They also learned who they were and the bottom line of their principles. As they emerged from the ashes of their devastating circumstances, they stepped up with strong character and the skills necessary to lead others through anything.

If there were a fifth element that these leaders share, it's their ongoing commitment to speak hope and healing into the lives of others. They have tasted some semblance of death and renewal, and they all have the passion to share what they've gained.

ABOUT THE AUTHOR

Writer • Director • Producer • Speaker

CJ Powers was raised in front of a motion picture camera. His love for the craft developed as he embraced his passion for telling stories. His admiration for peers and industry newbies drove him to start *CJ's Corner*, which can be found at:

http://cjpowersonline.com

Throughout his travel to 25+ countries over the past decade, CJ created his multicultural approach to screenwriting and conducted workshops worldwide. He has authored four books and has written numerous articles for magazines, newspapers, trade journals, blogs, e-newsletters, and e-zines.

CJ's films released internationally and television programs aired on CBS, PBS, ABC, the Family Channel, and various syndicated stations. The majority of CJ's directing awards, including the Silver CINDY and Crystal Communicator of Excellence, were for family films. He received additional honors from the U.S. and International Film and Video Festival and the New York Film Festival.

When CJ's not speaking on film, directing or screenwriting topics, he enjoys giving inspirational and motivational talks. His topics include: *Hope for the Holidays, Improving Your Future by Clearing Your Past, Drawing Out Your Man's Verbal Intimacy, Raising Media Wise Kids, G.U.T.S. – Guys/Gals Under Tremendous Stress,* and *I Can Do All Things.*

www.ingramcontent.com/pod-product-compliance
Lightning Source LLC
LaVergne TN
LVHW010606100826
845148LV00014B/2872

* 9 7 8 0 9 7 9 9 2 9 4 3 4 *